The Grass Ceiling

Eimear Ryan's writing has appeared in *Granta*, *Winter Papers*, the *Dublin Review* and the *Stinging Fly*. She is a co-founder of the literary journal *Banshee* and its publishing imprint, Banshee Press. Her first novel, *Holding Her Breath*, was shortlisted for the Newcomer of the Year Award at the Irish Book Awards and for the John McGahern Prize. *The Grass Ceiling* is her debut non-fiction book. A native of Co. Tipperary, Eimear now lives in Cork city.

The Grass Ceiling

On Being a Woman in Sport

EIMEAR RYAN

SANDYCOVE

an imprint of

PENGUIN BOOKS

SANDYCOVE

UK | USA | Canada | Ireland | Australia
India | New Zealand | South Africa

Sandycove is part of the Penguin Random House group of companies
whose addresses can be found at global.penguinrandomhouse.com.

First published 2023
001

Copyright © Eimear Ryan, 2023

The moral right of the author has been asserted

Set in 13.5/16pt Garamond MT Std
Typeset by Jouve (UK), Milton Keynes
Printed and bound in Great Britain by Clays Ltd, Elcograf S.p.A.

The authorized representative in the EEA is Penguin Random House Ireland,
Morrison Chambers, 32 Nassau Street, Dublin D02 YH68

A CIP catalogue record for this book is available from the British Library

ISBN: 978-1-844-88532-9

www.greenpenguin.co.uk

MIX
Paper from
responsible sources
FSC
www.fsc.org FSC® C018179

Penguin Random House is committed to a
sustainable future for our business, our readers
and our planet. This book is made from Forest
Stewardship Council® certified paper.

Do mo thuismitheoirí,
Ber & Séamus, le grá agus buíochas

Contents

Prologue: They Hurled Like Men

Imagine us in a shady stand on a hot summer's day, the whole family sat in a row: my father, Séamus; my mother, Bernadette; my older siblings, Conor and Eileen; and me. The cross-hatch of a Dairy Milk broken, the awkward sharing of eight squares among five. Imagine a few bottles of Scór cola; it was the nineties, after all.

We passed the programme back and forth as we waited for the game to start, and I often kept reading it even after the ball was thrown in. I was a bookish as well as a sporty child, better at reading text than the flow of the game unfolding below us. The programme flopped open to its stapled middle pages: the two teamsheets. Tipp and Cork, maybe, or Tipp and Clare. The Declan Ryan, Johnny Leahy, Skippy Cleary heyday. Then, a name I didn't recognize.

'Who's AN Other, Dad?'

My dad would get antsy at games; still does. Pitched forward, hands on his knees, as if barely able to hold himself back from the fray. He had played senior for Tipp in the luckless seventies, alongside icons like Eamon O'Shea, and was still deeply involved at club level; our summers consisted of traipsing along after him to an endless succession of matches and training sessions, our own hurleys in hand.

Engrossed in the game, he would've been startled at the interruption, but Dad is a teacher and a coach at heart.

'That means they're not sure who's starting in that position when they make the programme. The usual fella could be injured, maybe, so they might only decide on the day.'

AN Other. A placeholder from a time when managers were transparent about their lineups and their injury worries – a time before announcing your starting fifteen became a way to lure the opposing manager into a false assumption about your formation. Its use has fallen away, but the name – anonymous, other – has always stuck with me, in part because it captures something of how I've felt in the GAA for much of my life. Born into it, but not of it.

There was a strange androgyny to my childhood, obsessively pursuing a sport that was, back in the eighties and early nineties, very much a man's game. The summer I was three or four, I would answer only to 'Nicky', after Tipperary legend Nicky English. Around the time of my Holy Communion, I received a gift of a framed print of Seamus Redmond's famous poem 'The Hurler's Prayer', which I immediately added to my bedtime prayer rotation. The speaker of the poem appeals to God to give him all the attributes of the ideal hurler. It begins: *Grant me, O Lord, a hurler's skill, / with strength of arm and speed of limb.* As a child, I loved its rhyming couplets and accumulating rhythm. Even now it moves me, especially that daring turn in line 9 where the focus shifts abruptly to the afterlife: *When the final whistle for me is blown, / and I stand at last at God's judgement throne, / may the great referee when he calls my name / say 'You hurled like a man, you played the game.'* This is really how GAA people talk: everything in life – even death – is a hurling metaphor.

As a kid I used to stumble uncertainly over that last line, and another in the middle where the speaker wishes for his on-field actions to be 'manly'. I knew how to hurl, but the poem made me feel that manliness was the ultimate quality of a hurler, and I wasn't even sure what that meant. What did I know of hurling 'like a man'? What was the great referee going to say to me at the pearly gates? 'Sorry, you hurled like a girl; I can't let you in'?

The sport I play is called camogie. When I am abroad I describe it thus: it's a ball-and-stick game, a bit like hockey, a bit like lacrosse. Have you heard of hurling? I will sometimes ask. It's, like, the female version of that. No, it's basically the same sport. Yeah, I know it doesn't make sense.

As former Camogie Association president Joan O'Flynn memorably pointed out in the 2018 RTÉ documentary *The Game*, 'The verb is "to hurl".' In my mind I always think of the sport I play as hurling, even though the Camogie Association has been around almost as long as the Gaelic Athletic Association. To be a girl within Gaelic games is to grow up with a sort of dual consciousness. We are hurlers but we are also women, and have to navigate a sporting landscape that sometimes treats those identities as a contradiction. The Camogie Association is culturally linked to the GAA, but it is organizationally separate. Born in 1986, I grew up in a society that treated camogie as a secondary sport.

As players, we can be proud of our exploits and at the same time have completely internalized society's view of us. For example, if someone says to me, 'Tipp are playing on Sunday,' I will assume they are talking about the hurlers. My subconscious defaults to the men; I betray my own gender.

In this book, I have tried to be true to the ways that I think and the language that I use. I often use 'GAA' to signify not the Gaelic Athletic Association – the organization formed in 1884 to promote Gaelic games for boys and men only – but the whole cultural complex of Gaelic games. It is a culture I love, despite its sidelining of girls and women. And it is a culture that needs to change, as I hope this book will show.

When I was in primary school, I told my mother that my ambition was to play senior camogie for Tipperary and senior hurling for my club, Moneygall. I remember the delight in her response – the things kids come out with! – but also the caution, the worry. She let me down gently, explaining that I would most likely not have the physique to compete with men when I was older. Looking back now, I wonder if it was the first time she had to manage my expectations in relation to my gender.

I doubt that I paid much attention. I was as good as or better than a lot of the boys I played against. This has always formed a core part of my confidence as a player. Adolescence came and bodies changed, opening a gulf in size and strength. But my experience of hurling allows me to see that there's no mystique to men's sport.

By the time I was ten, I was equally comfortable hitting the ball on my right and left side. This was unusual at under-age levels, where a key tactic in marking was to 'force them on to their bad side'. It was my dad's doing, really: seeing that I was striking well on my left, he told me to practise on my right until it was just as good.

For a week, it was horribly frustrating, out at the gable end, throwing it up and missing it. That I was starting from square one was unusual: most right-handed hurlers learn to hit on their right side first, because you don't have to bring your hurley hand across your body. The right-hand swing is freer and more open for a right-handed hurler, just as the forehand is an easier tennis shot than the backhand. But I had grown comfortable on the more constricted left-hand side – the backhand – and didn't know what to do with the openness of the right. My first attempts were big loopy swings. Gradually, I began connecting more often than not. I had no control, no accuracy. But it's like anything: if you have enough time and enough patience to endure the frustration and discomfort of the initial failure, you will get there. And who has more time than a ten-year-old in rural Ireland?

I was lucky to have multiple outlets for my sporting passion: our burgeoning camogie club, founded in 1995; school, where boys and girls competed against each other on the pitch most lunchtimes; and the local boys' hurling team. At the time, organized camogie began at under-12, and so under-10 hurling was where I got my first proper competitive games. There were a handful of us girls deemed handy enough for hurling: myself, my cousins Mary Ryan and Maria Jones, and my friend and classmate Julie Kirwan.

In a small rural village where numbers were low, we were useful additions to the boys' team. I loved playing with the lads, and kept playing right through under-14 level, and even for an awkward, ill-advised year at under-16, togging out surreptitiously in the loo. Being good at hurling was like a secret pass into the mysterious and altogether more interesting world of boys, a way of overriding their pre-teen disdain for girls. They would say anything around me because I did not *count* as a girl. I once overheard a team-mate remark that I was 'some man', and didn't mind, because I knew he meant it as a compliment.

While the majority of my male teammates were nearly always supportive, the boys on opposing teams were some-times unsettled by the presence of girls on their pitch. You would see it in their gait as they came over to mark you, noticing the ponytail sticking out from under your helmet. First they'd be defensive and try to laugh it off, calling to their teammates: *Can you believe I'm marking a girl?* Once the game began and they realized you could play, their alarm would grow. Your prowess became an affront to them. I realized that for these boys, to have a girl get the better of them was the worst thing that could happen to them on the pitch.

They hurled like men. I've heard this phrase in one form or another since I was a child. I don't know if it was in gen-eral use before the publication of 'The Hurler's Prayer' in the 1960s, but given the sport's preoccupation with mas-culinity, I can only assume that it was. During the winter of 1996–7, when I had just turned ten, every day after school I alternated between two VHS tapes that I had recorded off the TV: the 1996 All-Ireland hurling final between Wexford and Limerick, and *Home Alone 2: Lost In New York.* The latter began a lifelong obsession with NYC;

the former was probably the first televised hurling match that I was truly captivated by – perhaps because I wasn't supporting either team, and could more easily grasp the beauty and symmetry and pathos of the game. I was starting to relate what I saw on the telly to what I did myself on the school pitch or at home out the back. One of the Wexford players performed an outrageous piece of business I'd never seen before: on a solo run, having caught the sliotar twice, he handpassed it on to the ground in front of himself and picked it up again, thus resetting the catch count. I practised this move endlessly on our front lawn, but never had the nerve to try it in real life.

The Wexford players – many of them mustachioed – were dear to me. Some – Billy Byrne and George O' Connor – seemed old, though they were the same age then as I am now. 'This is our day in the sun, we're not going to not walk the full round of the pitch,' said Liam Griffin, Wexford's manager that year, motivating his players ahead of All-Ireland final day. 'We're walking with our heads up . . . Stand up like soldiers, this is a man's game, stand up there, can we stand up like men in front of the President, can we stand up and show a bit of respect and then get out and put the lights on to green . . . and let's go.'

A man's game. You hear this sort of thing even now, more often than you'd think, from pundits and commentators; some of my favourite hurling minds, in fact. An emotional Michael Duignan tweet, after a promising 2018 performance from Offaly: 'They hurled like men.' Davy Fitzgerald on RTÉ's *Morning Ireland* in 2021, discussing the ins and outs of the advantage rule: 'It's a manly game.'

(Speaking on the same issue, Brendan Cummins did not bring gender into it: 'It's a free-flowing game.')

This is not at all to say that Griffin, Duignan and Fitzgerald are sexist. By now, I know what they're getting at. They're invoking the traits of positive masculinity; to hurl like a man means to hurl with strength, courage, integrity, honesty, resilience. But this language excludes women, and seems to suggest (intentionally or not) that camogie players can't access such qualities. In popular discourse we hurl like men, but throw like a girl, gossip like women, cry like a little girl. You do not hear of people aspiring to hurl like women.

Fitzgerald recently coached the Cork camogie team, and I fondly remember him as a guest coach with Tipperary camogie in the early noughts: challenging, electrifying sessions. While managing the Wexford hurlers, Fitzgerald brought in Mags Darcy, the All-Ireland winning camogie goalie, as a goalkeeping coach. 'There's no gender with Davy,' Darcy remarked at the time, meaning her being a woman was not seen as an impediment for the job. This is the arena of sport. Maleness is elevated, aspirational; femaleness is overlooked, or forgiven.

So where does that leave us camogie players? Do we simply need to magnify our masculine streaks, much like men talk about exploring their feminine sides? Or are the qualities we're alluding to here – passion, aggression, courage – actually universal and gender-neutral? One might argue that traditionally feminine traits – gentleness, sensitivity, passivity – are of little use on the hurling field. But others, like cooperation, communication and empathy, *are* essential to being part of a team. Hurling is soft as well as hard, graceful as well as furious. It is as much dance as it is fight.

'You're the best girl hurler I ever met,' a boy told me the summer I went to the Kerry Gaeltacht. I was twelve at the time and had a hopeless crush on him; I thought I could impress him with my hurling prowess. I was not yet aware of the unspoken rule, that I was supposed to let *him* impress *me* and not the other way around. But at night, I turned the phrase *best girl hurler* over and over in my mind, as if it was a prize.

1. Boys, Oh Boys

When I remember my grandfather, I think of his para-
phernalia: the trilby hat that was worn summer and winter;
the pipe, which he reluctantly gave up in his seventies; the
walking stick; the rattling typewriter; the Pioneer pin on
his lapel.

I do something similar with Julia, my grandmother on
my mother's side. Whenever I sit in the mid-century arm-
chair I inherited from her, or change the date on her
perpetual calendar, I think of her. I don't own any of my
grandfather's personal effects. But I do have a copy of each
of his books, and his memory card watches over me from
the noticeboard above my desk.

When a great character exits, we're left with the props.

Séamus Ó Riain (1916–2007), my grandfather, was a teacher,
sportsperson, writer, administrator, Gaeilgeoir, gardener
and historian. He played Junior hurling and football for
Tipperary and was an accomplished track and field athlete,
specializing in the long jump and races of 220 and 440
yards, known as the two-twenty and the four-forty. In my
family, he's our origin story – the GAA lightning rod from
which we all caught a spark. He is still somehow the notional
head of the family. His anniversary Mass has eclipsed
Christmas as the annual family occasion at which I will reli-
ably catch up with most of my aunts, uncles and cousins.

It may seem strange to begin a book about being a woman in sport with a portrait of a patriarch, but it couldn't have begun any other way.

He served as President of the GAA from 1967 to 1970. During his tenure, Tipperary lost the All-Ireland hurling final twice. Sometimes I'll catch him in archive footage on *Reeling in the Years* or *Up for the Match*, dapper in a three-piece suit, handing over the Liam MacCarthy Cup with a tight smile.

We are lucky to have the footage. He also featured in an episode of *I Live Here*, an RTÉ documentary series from the late eighties. I was too young at the time to remember it being filmed, but throughout my childhood the video was a source of wonder to me. It's very surreal to see the familiar reframed for a wider audience. There's Nana and Grandad strolling up their well-tended garden, chatting. There's my dad in his Buddy Holly glasses. My mam in her beloved classroom. My older brother Conor, about eight or nine at the time, out hurling on the school pitch.

After my grandfather died, my cousin Eamonn transferred the episode from VHS on to DVD for all ten branches of the family. Séamus would have approved. He was the village's amateur historian, and whenever Americans came to Moneygall looking for their roots they were sent to his house on Main Street. He died in January 2007, about ten months before the Irish roots of Barack Obama, then a presidential candidate, were traced to Moneygall. Séamus would have got an almighty kick out of that. 'Boys, oh boys,' he would have said, his ready phrase for almost any situation – an expression of pathos, surprise, wonder, but most usually glee. Now, at family gatherings, all we have to do to invoke him is say the words: *Boys, oh boys.*

He was a teetotaller who had a cheerful attitude to drink, often pouring a full tumbler of whiskey for guests in a show of hospitality, not really knowing what a typical serving size looked like. He knew the words to 'Auld Lang Syne' and would insist on staying up until midnight every New Year's Eve, to join crossed hands with whoever happened to be around.

His speech had the quality of the written word, eloquent and efficient. 'There is no final history,' he said on *I Live Here*, when asked whether his book *Dunkerrin: A Parish in Ely O'Carroll* was the definitive history of his locality. When I interviewed him about his role in founding the youth GAA tournament Féile na nGael – which to this day remains an important marker in the careers of young hurlers – he said wryly: 'Success has many fathers, but failure is an orphan.'

His wit was ever-present, lurking beneath his carefully chosen words, even in the unlikeliest of circumstances. At my grandmother Mary's removal in 1997, a former Tipperary hurler named Mickey 'The Rattler' Byrne, a stout corner-back from the forties and fifties, came up to him for handshakes and reminiscences. Séamus stood with his five sons as the old hurler said his piece. 'The GAA know how to bury their people with dignity,' said the Rattler, before shuffling away. Once he was out of earshot, Séamus turned to his sons. 'That same fella buried many a corner-forward *without* dignity.'

I starkly remember him entering the house during a rare visit from my uncle Martin on my mother's side, who emigrated to New Zealand at eighteen. 'God save all here,' Séamus said at the threshold. It was a phrase he occasionally used, but I also wondered if it was something of a rebuke. This is what you gave up, he seemed to be saying: this old deep culture, this rootedness.

The parish of Dunkerrin straddles the zigzag border between Tipperary and Offaly; like many parishes, it ignores town and county boundaries. Dunkerrin village is in Offaly, as is Moneygall village, but a sliver of Tipperary lies in between, and this contains both the local GAA grounds and my family home. I would have supported Tipp anyway – my father, uncles and grandfather had played for Tipp; my mother was from the parish of Killenaule, in the south of the county – but I was still grateful that our house was technically on blue and gold territory. I was keenly aware of when our car would cross the various boundaries, smug in my tiny Tipp peninsula.

In Moneygall, we Ryans are numerous and devoted to hurling. You don't get much choice in the matter; it is ingrained. My dad and his brothers were part of the last legendary Moneygall senior hurling team that won back-to-back Tipperary senior county titles in 1975 and 1976. We have not won any such titles since, but hurling continues to be Moneygall's favourite pastime.

My first hurley was a 28-inch cut down to a more manageable size. My father told me that a good hurley should be an extension of my arm. I started on the front lawn, drop-hitting a tennis ball off the wall, gradually improving until I was admitted to play with my two older siblings. Many times we broke the small toilet window and had to drive to the hardware shop in Roscrea for replacement panes of glass. Once, I broke it twice in one day. My dad never raised his voice.

Hurleys accumulate. The shed at home is a graveyard of them and I can trace my playing career through them: sticks of various lengths, grubby with use, cracked and fissured, carefully wound with insulating tape in club colours.

My grandfather seemed to preside over all of it. He always stood at the same spot on the sideline of Moneygall hurling field, leaning forward against the diagonal wall that funnelled spectators into the entrance of the stand, watching matches or training from under the brim of his trilby hat. He had thirty-nine grandchildren: twenty-one boys and eighteen girls. Of his grandsons, eighteen pursued Gaelic games to some extent; of his granddaughters, just seven. Much of this was down to opportunity: while there were clubs, school teams and other grassroots structures ready to receive my male cousins born in the sixties and seventies, the same can't be said for my older female cousins. It's an imperfect but telling data set: in one extended GAA-mad family, the boys were more than twice as likely to play as the girls.

At Dunkerrin National School, where my siblings and I went, our father was the principal. Dad was eager that both boys and girls participate in hurling; his only distinction between the sexes was his insistence that the girls wear helmets. I still remember the strangeness of my first helmet, a bulbous blue Mycro: the rattle of it, no matter how tightly fastened. In the early nineties, they weren't really made for children's heads. We tottered around the pitch like astronauts, disproportioned and off-balance.

I played by two codes – one set of rules with the boys' hurling team, and another with the camogie club, founded the year I turned eight. Camogie seemed strange to me from the start, like a parallel-universe version of hurling: essentially the same, but with a handful of inexplicable differences. There were peculiar position names ('centre-centre') that sounded funny when we said them out loud. You weren't allowed to expose the steel band of the bas in case of injury, so most players had a roll of insulating tape in their gear bag to apply fresh tape before each match, or at least to patch over any gaps where the previous game's tape had worn away. Our O'Neill's togs – the shorts I wore while playing with the boys – had to be covered up with skirts. Our club had a bag of one-size-fits-all wraparound skirts that had to be worn by everyone from under-12s up to Junior: another strange pre-match routine, safety-pinning our skirts in place. A few minutes before each game were taken up with these rituals of concealment.

Many of the rule differences seemed like needless concessions to the supposed weakness and inferior skill of women. You could handpass a goal, a move that had been banned in hurling since the 1980s; you could drop the hurley, which was a foul in hurling; you were not allowed to jostle an opponent (although depending on the ref, you might get away with it); and you could catch the ball three times in possession instead of two. I prided myself on not utilizing the camogie rule-loopholes in case I developed 'bad habits' that would affect my hurling career.

These rules had existed in some form since the Camogie Association was founded in 1904, presumably because women were considered incapable of playing hurling in

all its untrammelled physicality. Even the sport's name is
a diminutive – derived from *camóg*, a smaller version of
the *camán* or hurley. As the historian Paul Rouse wrote in
the *Irish Examiner*, 'It says much for the nature of Irish
society and its sporting world that the establishment of
associations for women to play hurling and Gaelic football could only be undertaken under the disguise of
different names. Apparently, it would be an affront to the
manliness of the Irish male that Irish women should actually be considered capable of playing the same game as
them. Such an affront would devalue not just the worth of
men, but also the games that they played . . . the very fact
of the name is the product of a time and a mode of
thought that presented women as incapable, unworthy
and – ultimately – justly unequal.'

One thread in the history of camogie has been the slow,
gradual unpicking of these feminized rules. Today, the
camogie rulebook is almost totally in alignment with hurling's. In 2021, the handpass goal and the hurley-drop were
officially phased out, while the jostle was finally given the
green light.

But in the nineties, when I was a child, we still laboured
under the vestiges of the old camogie rulebook. Even
worse, the camogie matches I played drew a fraction of
the crowds that my hurling matches did. I felt a sense of
unfairness and confusion at this, as well as a tacit accept-
ance born of experience and internalized sexism: camogie
just wasn't as *good* as hurling, was it? Not as physical, ham-
pered by its own silly rules, largely ignored by the general
public. Even as a kid I realized that for a female player
there would be no glamour, no social capital. We only saw

camogie players on TV once a year, and they were rarely in the papers – never a picture to cut out or a poster for the wall.

Almost every player in our fledgling camogie club was of my generation, though I did have a handful of elders. My uncle Jack's wife, Orla, won three camogie All-Irelands with Dublin in the 1970s. Their daughter, my cousin Naoise, who was about ten years older than me, was a talented camogie player herself. They lived in Dublin, though, and I never got to see them play, so most of my role models and heroes – Nicky English, Pat Fox, Michael Cleary, D. J. Carey – were male. The GAA-adjacent women I knew seemed to get all the thankless tasks, without which the organization would grind to a halt: washing jerseys, giving lifts, putting dinners on the table after training. My female teammates and I didn't want those roles for ourselves; we wanted what the lads had.

This was how I grew up. Summer camps. Roll-lifting competitions. Trips to Mosney for Community Games long puck. Seven-a-side blitzes. Autograph books in Semple Stadium. The soothing monotony of hitting the ball against the gable end, over and over, as far as the summer dusk will take you.

My grandfather was a writer and, because of him, I thought from an early age that I could be a writer too. His front room in Main Street, Moneygall was lined with floor-to-ceiling bookshelves containing mostly history books, but also lots of poetry, Shakespeare and canonical novels. He was unapologetically intellectual and supportive of the arts. Even in retirement, he worked daily at a rattly old typewriter, and later at a desktop PC which he openly despised. Though I didn't realize it at the time, he was a model for me – someone with a writing practice, who showed me that being a writer wasn't some lofty calling, but a daily grind.

He wrote speeches, essays, histories, even an epic ballad called 'Roast Ham', about an intrepid pig that meets an unfortunate end. As a child I learned it off by heart so that I would have a party piece in the back pocket. For my Leaving Cert history project, I drew extensively on his second book, a biography of the GAA's first president, Maurice Davin. My project was about the IRA's use of the GAA as a recruitment ground in its early years. It is revealing that Davin was the GAA founder Séamus was drawn to – not the larger-than-life, bolshy Michael Cusack, nor the Tipperary Fenian J. K. Bracken, after whom a nearby GAA club in Templemore is named. Davin was mild-mannered, abstemious, pacifist and ethically without reproach. For this, he was hounded out of office.

In 2016, my father found and transcribed a diary among my grandfather's school papers, written half in Irish, half in English. It dates from September to December 1938, when Séamus was twenty-two and living on the tiny island of Gorumna, off the coast of Connemara. He was teaching on the even tinier island of Inishbarra, a job to which he was rowed each morning; if the weather was bad, school was cancelled.

The diary – or the *cinnlae* as it's come to be known in my family – gives an insight into the intense young person Séamus was: observant, ambitious, hard on himself, and delightfully catty on occasion. For me, it was a revelation, an intimate insight into a person I admired and wanted to know better.

Some of his concerns are the familiar ones of youth, regardless of the era: work and financial pressures, and a longing for life to finally get going. 'I'm just after sealing another of those application packets,' he writes. 'It's terribly distressing – filling in the same old thing over and over again, trying to change the wording of application to make it look or sound better . . . trying to persuade myself that this is surely *the* lucky one.'

He came of age in a time when far-right forces were rising internationally, and those anxieties populate the pages. In the diary's first entry, written during the annexing of the Sudetenland, he writes: 'Hitler seems to have many of the qualities of a child.' Later, he is alarmed by a book recommendation on a trip to Galway: 'The librarian, seeing I liked travel or adventure seemingly, offered me Eoin O'Duffy's *Crusade in Spain* . . . I shall read it out of courtesy.'

His politics are discernible, too, in his commentary on the island itself. He wasn't at all sentimental about the islanders and their way of life, which was primitive even by 1930s standards, but recognized the hardship they endured. Describing the islanders' typical diet, he writes: 'Bread and tea for breakfast. Flour bought in shops at a high price . . . Homemade butter while it lasts. Thus jam – as Irish Creamery Butter is too expensive. Just imagine the finest butter in the world denied to those where it is produced . . . Bacon maybe once a week and this despite the fact that pigs are fattened on this farm . . . In a country rich in farm produce, the most nourishing of this produce is denied the ordinary folk.'

He never made it known what party he was voting for in any election. (In this, he contrasted with my grandmother Mary who, having lost her uncle Jack Collison to anti-Treaty forces in 1922, was a staunch Fine Gaeler.) He was approached by political parties at different times in his life and asked to run, but never took them up on it.

At my grandfather's removal, my then-boss sought me out in the throngs. When he found me, I was in fits of laughter – cracking up at something one of my cousins had said. I remember him looking at me slightly askance and later I realized that it probably wasn't a good look, laughing hysterically at a family funeral. But when my grandfather brought us together, it was always a good time.

For me, the first sombre moment came in the funeral home, just before the coffin was to be closed. The undertaker asked that everyone who was not family leave. This didn't exactly clear the room. There were ten children, their spouses, three dozen grandchildren, and a handful of great-grandchildren too. One of my older cousins went to the coffin and kissed Séamus on the forehead and went out the door, and we all followed suit.

Among so many grandchildren, it was sometimes difficult to get Séamus's attention, to bask in its full glow. As a kid, especially, I did what I could to get it. After Mass on Sundays, we'd walk up the street to Nana and Grandad's for freshly baked scones and sausages, and I remember pretending to prefer brown scones to white, knowing that would get me Séamus's huff of approval.

I didn't cry until after the funeral, when I'd gotten the J. J. Kavanagh bus from Moneygall back to my room at

Dublin City University, where I was then in my third year of studies. I remember howling into my pillow that night once I was on my own again. His death wasn't a tragedy. He was ninety and for most of those years he'd been in good physical and mental health. But at the same time I knew that my home and family were changed now, indelibly, and that all our lives would be poorer without him.

My dad, also named Séamus, recently said to me: 'I knew about five versions of him.' When Dad was young, he said, Séamus was a strict disciplinarian. Over the years their relationship mellowed and by the time of Séamus's death, they were close, but it has stuck with me, this idea of my grandfather as a chameleon. Maybe that's the hallmark of a great, multi-faceted, complex person – they are constantly evolving.

Dad once told me that the only time he ever remembers hugging Séamus was in Semple Stadium in 1975, at the final whistle, when Moneygall won its first ever county title. My dad was in his mid-twenties, shaggy-haired, playing at wing-forward that day. Séamus was not quite sixty, just settling into his grandfatherly gravitas, overjoyed at witnessing the first major title for his club. When I think about that hug, I still feel a tightness in my throat. Whatever might be said about the GAA, it's been a conduit so many times for Irish men to express their emotions: joy, hope, despair, even love.

In 1997, I was picked to play in the Cumann na mBunscol Mini 7s demonstration match at half-time in the All-Ireland final. Tipp were playing Clare in the senior game, and Jamesie O'Connor would break my ten-year-old heart by pucking the winning point into the Nally Stand, where I sat, in the game's dying moments. But before all that, I got to run out on the pitch myself.

Any memory I had of the experience has mostly been displaced by the television footage that I, a tiny narcissist, would watch over and over later: I won a puck-out near the sideline, rounded my marker, was blocked down, and took an indifferent line-ball. I don't remember being aware of the huge crowd, or what it sounded like, or whether I was excited or calm.

One moment, though, I remember with almost perfect clarity. As a former GAA president, my grandfather got the best tickets in the house for All-Ireland finals: upholstered seats dead-centre of the Hogan Stand, near where the cup was presented. Coming off the pitch, I bent to pick a fistful of grass, which I later put in a ziplock bag and kept until it crisped up. As I walked towards the tunnel, I looked up to see if I could see Grandad. There he was, a couple of rows from the front, sitting next to my uncle Eugene. I waved. He caught my eye and beamed. I forget most of my ten minutes on the sod in Croke Park, what it felt like, but I remember this: the shadow of the approaching tunnel and, above, my grandfather waving.

2. The Field

I grew up in an L-shaped bungalow on the N7 between Moneygall and Dunkerrin, two tiny villages straddling the Tipperary–Offaly border. The house was built in 1977, meitheal-style, with friends and neighbours – many of them my dad's teammates on the hurling team – helping out by digging foundations and building walls and laying slates. I love the photographs from that time, square and saturated with age: hurlers up on the roof, steering wheelbarrows, taking breaks with sandwiches and flasks of tea balanced on hay bales. The house sits on half an acre of gardens tended by my parents, including three large lawns, an extensive vegetable patch, and mature trees. There are two oak trees that my father, a forward-thinker, grew from acorns in the year 2000, now over twenty feet tall.

It was an idyllic environment for a kid, and it's only now, living in a terraced house in Cork city with a tiny patio out back, that I recognize how privileged I was to grow up that way. No wonder I was handy at a young age: right on my doorstep I had the space to endlessly practise, to solo the length of a pitch, to open the shoulders, to let fly.

I drive north once a month or so to visit my parents. The surroundings have changed utterly since I was a kid. In the 1990s, Moneygall was a three-pub, six-shop village, clustered around one long, curving street and surrounded by farmland. With the completion of the M7 motorway in

2010, most traffic now bypasses Moneygall completely, making the main road on which my parents' home sits much quieter and safer but also deadening the village. Main Street used to funnel all the Dublin–Limerick traffic; now you can drive through the village and not meet another car.

When I was a kid, it was a straight run to the hurling field from our house: less than a kilometre as the crow flies. I used to walk there in the summertime with my hurley and a bag of sliotars to practise free-taking or to workshop different goal-scoring scenarios. I campaigned unsuccessfully to be allowed to cycle there, the volume of traffic being considered too dangerous. Most often we drove, especially if we had training gear with us, a spin of maybe thirty seconds in the car.

It is all changed now. A large roundabout sits between the bungalow and the hurling field, a cog in the machinery of the national infrastructure offering slip roads to Limerick, the village itself, and the Obama Plaza, a large petrol station that opened in 2014. While I remember there being two petrol pumps in the village in my youth, there had not been an option to buy petrol locally for many years. Before the Plaza, there had never been an ATM in Moneygall either, or a chipper, or an off-licence. The Plaza brought these amenities but it also effectively killed most other small businesses in the village: Bergin's, the grocery and deli at which I worked as a teenager, and Donovan's, a convenience store adjoining the funeral home. Now, as you drive from my parents' house to the hurling field, you will pass life-size bronze statues of the Obamas facing the road, holding hands and waving. The day they visited

Moneygall in 2011, their helicopter landed – where else? – on the hurling pitch.

Over the Christmas break in 2021, I drive to the field to meet my sister Eileen and her kids, who are ten, eight and five. The main entrance gate is locked so we park at the road and retrieve our hurleys and sliotars out of our respective boots. I've played my hurling with a club in Cork for the last five years, and I can't remember the last time I was in the field. The kids want to practise penalties; I'm recovering from injury and want to see how it feels to be back on a pitch. We're all experimenting.

The field itself is now a different place than the one where I grew up playing. The long straight driveway into the field curves to the left, wrapping around the endline. In my youth this driveway was gravelled and potholed; my dad would swivel to avoid the dips as he drove us in. Now, it's been upgraded with room for two cars to pass comfortably.

I stand in goals at the village end as my nieces and nephew mercilessly ping balls at me. There's a new high net behind the goals; when I was a kid, we relied instead on the branches of a huge sycamore tree to stop the balls going into the neighbouring field. Now the tree is gone. The five-foot wall that separated the pitch proper from the driveway – a wall that I could never see over, that seemed designed to keep children out, or in – has since been replaced by a green post-and-rail fence.

Now the kids want to practise their long striking, so I'm relieved of goalkeeping duties. We move out to the half-way line. The high bank that runs along the old N7, and the dugouts that I remember being built in the nineties, remain the same. A new digital scoreboard sits within a concrete maintenance shed. Shooting into the Dunkerrin end, I hit wide after wide; the ball drops short; my touch is off. The kids run rings around me.

The stand, built in the seventies, holds numerous sensory memories for me. Very rarely did I actually sit down and watch a match there; when I was older and capable of concentrating on a game, I preferred to stand on the bank on the opposite side. But the stand, like so many other unlikely sites around the community – the old Church of Ireland graveyard, the vendors' arches in Dunkerrin – was a makeshift playground. The steel railings that flanked the stand became monkey bars. There are photos of me hanging off these railings with my cousins; three of us in a contorted row. The concrete seating strips created 'lanes' for us to race each other. We raced between the seats, on the seats, jumping from one to the other until we reached the top. We pucked against the back wall of the stand while standing on the seating. We broke the skin of our knees open many times.

The small diagonal wall that was my grandfather's vantage spot remains. The clubhouse itself – containing dressing-rooms, meeting rooms, and a racquetball alley – now bears his name. But the biggest change is the second pitch, positioned to the south of the original field and elevated above it. I trained on it when it was a raw, pock-marked stretch of thready grass with temporary goalposts. Now it's match-ready.

By the time we walk back to the cars, spent, I am limping again.

*

Despite the fact that we lived so close to Moneygall village, my brother, sister and I attended Dunkerrin primary school, three miles in the opposite direction. This was where my parents taught. A three-classroom, three-teacher school when I started, it gained another teacher halfway through my schooling, and has had a significant extension built since. It was the type of school where you knew every single pupil by name. There were eight in my class.

I was taught by my parents for four out of my eight years of primary school. Mrs Ryan was universally beloved, so that was easy, but my dad was the principal and therefore the disciplinarian, and it became socially awkward in fifth and sixth class when he gave out to my friends. In Junior Infants I had trouble separating Mr Ryan's school persona from his dad identity. There were a couple of incidents when I ran up to him in the Seomra Mór, with most of the school assembled, and hugged him around the knees. After I was gently sat down and given a talking to, I briefly believed that my father and the principal were in fact two separate entities: alter egos, like the superhero cartoons I watched on *The Den* after school.

At breaktimes, left to our own devices, we mostly played soccer. We could play on the basketball court, and only one person needed to remember to bring a ball, whereas hurling required all of us to be organized: hurley, helmet, boots, tracksuit bottoms for the muddy pitch. That said, it was a primary school rite of passage to play in the school hurling league. From second class upwards, anyone interested in hurling – boys and girls alike – could participate. Captains would be selected from fifth and sixth class and all other interested players would be randomly allocated to a team. For a lot of us, it was our introduction to competitive, organized sport, and we approached the lunchtime fixtures as if walking out on to Croke Park.

We had two sets of jerseys – the red school set (every captain's first choice) and a maroon set of mysterious origin. The maroon jerseys were well-worn and oversized, falling sometimes to the knees of the Rang a Dó players. They had strange orange patches on them resembling lens flare, as if they'd been bleached in the sun.

It's only recently, in a chat with my dad and my uncle Philip, that I discovered the esteemed provenance of those maroon jerseys: they were used by the Moneygall senior team up until the 1960s, at which point the club colours changed. The story goes that one of the lads was away at boarding school in Kilkenny, where the school jerseys were black and red. His school gear was so admired when he came back to hurl for Moneygall in the summer that the club decided to change their colours to match.

I love this story because it demonstrates the charmingly accidental nature of club colours. To this day, I have a deep affinity for the colours black and red: it always makes me smile to see them together. But if things had gone a different way, I would have the same Pavlovian response towards maroon and white instead.

As a Tipp woman, I love the blue and gold, and considered it a good omen that my adoptive club in Cork, St Finbarr's Barrs, has the same colours. But the Tipp colours are also somewhat arbitrary, adopted since 1925 from the Tubberadora club (now Boherlahan), who were county champions at the time. Prior to that, the Tipp team changed jerseys each year to reflect the colours of the reigning county champions – hence the now-famous white and green Bloody Sunday shirt, taken from the Grangemockler jersey. Even Cork's blood and bandage has an accidental origin: when their original blue jerseys were confiscated by British soldiers in 1919, they borrowed the shirts of the Father O'Leary Temperance Association team, and have been red ever since.

After school I'd run up to the arches in Dunkerrin village, where most of the kids were collected. While we waited, we'd buy penny sweets in Byrnes's shop or dare each other to jump off the biggest tombs in the Church of Ireland graveyard. Everything was a competition to me back then; I wanted to be the best, even at spelling tests. Even at tomb-jumping.

My after-school activities included music (keyboard, tin whistle, bodhrán); Irish dancing, at which I diligently learned the steps but had little talent; and sport. The parish had an athletics club – St Flannan's – as well as a GAA club, and I competed in both track and field and cross-country until my mid-teens. Athletics taught me about losing, about grit, about the power of teamwork. I was – am – a heavy-footed runner, never the fastest on the track, and with a tendency to plough up the muddy cross-country field instead of skipping over it like some of my more light-footed teammates.

We trained for cross-country in Byrnes's field, halfway between my house and Dunkerrin. I went to school with the six Byrne kids and would later play camogie with Bríd, one of the best cross-country runners St Flannan's ever produced. I felt like I got to know every blade of grass of that field: every slope, every wet patch, every rewarding stretch of downhill. We were always preceded by clouds of our own breath. On nights when it was very dark, Bríd's mother Sarah-Anne would drive her car into the furthest corner and switch on the headlights. There was an old graveyard there, too, and at Halloween the Byrnes would adorn the graves with blow-up skeletons and plastic pumpkins.

Cross-country was a slog, or character-building as my parents would have it. We ran barefoot as under-10s before graduating to spikes. The meets were held at roped-off fields recently vacated by livestock. There was always cow dung on the ground. There was always a hill. The start of a race was a frantic fight for space, runners elbowing and stepping on each other. ('She got spiked' was an oft-repeated phrase at these meets.) Near the finish-line the route narrowed, leading you into a roped-off chute, ensuring that the runners finished in single file and places could be counted. You would be handed a raffle ticket indicating your finishing spot. I was never in the medals but sometimes I finished in the top twenty or thirty or forty, and that helped our team performance. Afterwards you would find the patch of grass where your club had set up camp, towel off, change out of your wet clothes, get your tracksuit on, eat whatever snacks you brought from home, shout on your clubmates in other races. There was no glamour in cross-country – no lovely flourish of skill, no perfectly executed set-pieces, no last-minute goal to win the game. The only way out was through.

I was a talented child hurler, but there were two problems. One was that I was very short-sighted. I wore glasses

to see the board in school, and by the time I was competing on the hurling pitch I could only judge where the ball
was by the movement of the other players. In sixth class, I
went up to Dublin with my mother to get fitted for soft
contact lenses. It took me half an hour the first time to
coax them on to my eyeballs, but the reward was exhilarating. I pointed at a bus parked across the street from the
optometrist's office in Ballsbridge: 'I can read the ads on
the bus!' It was shocking to me that other people had been
going around with these enhanced powers of perception
all along. Now that I could see the ball coming, I was able
to get there first.

The second problem was that I was afraid. This became
apparent early on: for all my ability, there were certain
aspects of the game for which I lacked the necessary
courage. Clash balls, for one: I would hang back, flinch,
dreading the sting of hurleys colliding, the shock up my
arm. I tried to practise blocking down with a friend one
day. Similar thing: she would throw the ball up, and I
would close my eyes, bracing myself, and half-heartedly
reach in, fully expecting a slap on the hand or the sting of
the ball somewhere on my body. When I opened my eyes,
she was laughing. She hadn't even swung at it. 'You need
to get in closer,' she said.

It's one of the first counter-intuitive lessons you learn in
hurling: the closer you are, the safer you are. None of this
has ever come naturally to me. Even now, more than two
decades later, I still have to persuade myself to get into the
thick of the action. Most of my mental preparation in the
week before a match involves picturing myself catching
high balls, blocking down full-backs, winning clashes. If

I'm at a low ebb, or stressed about something else in my life, this will be the first facet of my game to go. But if I'm on form, I'll pick balls from the air with abandon; and because it's so hard for me, nothing gives me a greater thrill.

This is the only way I know how to be brave: by being afraid first, then working in the opposite direction.

A significant fact about my early education is that I was taught to sing 'The Offaly Rover' but not 'Slievenamon'. I attended Scoil Muire Dunkerrin from 1990 to 1998, and in that time Offaly won two All-Ireland hurling titles while Tipp won only one. When Tipp won in 1991, I was a Senior Infant, too young to realize how rare All-Irelands are, how they must be milked and celebrated to the nth degree.

My classmates were split between Tipp and Offaly allegiances. There may even have been more Offaly supporters than Tipp, to judge by the county jerseys worn on PE days: Carroll's Meats outnumbered Finches significantly. My Offaly classmates lorded their successes over me – as I would have over them, if Tipp's fortunes had been better – and I grew up with a slight inferiority complex; 'the Faithful County' sounded much nobler and more substantial than Tipp's nickname (what did 'the Premier' even mean?).

Just after I went into third class, Offaly won their famous 'five-minute final', in which they scored an unanswered 2–5 in the space of five minutes, pulling back a five-point Limerick lead. After this feat, it was inevitable that we would be taught to sing Offaly's song. The lyrics are still embedded in my brain with those other songs of primary school, churning together with 'Zacchaeus', 'The Apostles' and the '30 days has September' rhyme. I still remember the way a classroom of eight-year-olds wavered and cracked on the high notes: *At ClonmacNOISE I'll see you* . . . Even now I'm not sure of my own county's anthem, and stumble on 'Slievenamon' when it's sung on the terraces. After that great opening surge of 'Alone, all alone', I quickly lose track.

Dunkerrin parish, from which Moneygall GAA club draws its players, is situated mostly in Offaly, with two small nodes of land overlapping into Tipp. This means that a large section of the club's pool of players are Offaly supporters, yet Moneygall plays its hurling in the Tipperary championship.

I grew up with a keen awareness not just of county borders but of parish boundaries, those dotted lines on old Ordnance Survey maps. I knew if I took a left in Moneygall village and kept going up Army Hill past my grandmother Julia's house, I'd eventually find myself in Toomevara territory. Toom is a slightly larger village a five-minute drive away; they were our nearest neighbours and dearest foes. Our mutual disdain was like that of Springfield and Shelbyville or Pawnee and Eagleton – with Moneygall in the Springfield/Pawnee role of scrappy underdog. (Toom tops the roll of honour with thirty-three Tipperary North titles, while Moneygall's 1975 title stands alone.)

One life, one club, one border, two counties. Boundaries and their associated allegiances seemed constantly in flux. I had friends, cousins and teammates on Moneygall club teams that became rivals as soon as schools fixtures started up. My school, Dunkerrin NS, was full of rural farming kids and had a strong Offaly streak; Moneygall NS, from their cosmopolitan perch in the village, called us 'the Kernies'. Our jerseys were even the inverse of each other: ours red and black, theirs black and red. We were the same, but different, constantly defining ourselves by what we were and, perhaps more importantly, by what we weren't.

It's comical, because we all grew up more or less the same way. We were isolated. We had no public transport and many of our homes were ringed by farmland. Discos, cinemas and swimming pools all required a willing adult to give a lift there and back. Dial-up internet and imported TV shows set in American high schools gave us some glimpse of the wider world, but mostly we were in our back yards, hurleys in hand, methodically pucking until the last of the light.

We all learned the same myths, too. Hurling was not only the fastest field game in the world (*the ball travels at speeds of up to 120 mph*) but also the oldest (*references to the sport have been found in Brehon laws dating back to the fifth century*). We learned how Cúchulainn got his name. How GAA players are not men, but giants. The notion that hurling was better – *purer* – than other sports was planted early, without us ever realizing it. Needless to say, all the figures in this mythology and iconography were male. This I accepted as if it were the natural order of things.

In the summers, my siblings and I spent most of our time outdoors, pursuing different sports. We had dogs, a long succession of spaniels and Labradors, who we were free to take for walks in the hills and woods behind the house. If we were feeling ambitious, we might go all the way to the tower, a folly built in the early nineteenth century by the landlord at Busherstown House on the highest point of his land – all the better to look down on the surrounding peasants. To get there, we had to cross a stream, find our way over multiple hedges, navigate herds of cows and sheep, our shins grazed by the long grass. The tower had a crumbling spiral staircase inside that led up to a viewing point at the faux-battlements – a staircase that we were forbidden to climb, lest it give way beneath us. The last time I was there, a few Christmases ago with my nieces, nephew and stepson, only the bottom few rungs of the staircase remained.

We aped the sports we saw on TV. Eileen was into gymnastics, an obsession born from watching the exploits of Romanian teenager Lavinia Miloşovici at the 1992 Barcelona Olympics. In place of leotards, we wore long-sleeved t-shirts under swimsuits; a plank strung across two buckets was our balance beam; the back lawn was where we performed our floor routines. In June, we would chalk the lines of a tennis court on the big expanse of concrete out the back, using the pole that propped up the washing line as a giant ruler.

And then there was the freedom of the many local hurling fields where we went to watch matches: Toomevara, Cloughjordan, Nenagh, Borrisoleigh. My cousins and I marauding in packs. Climbing up on scoreboards. Buying sweets from the white cloth-covered trestle tables at the corner of the pitch, coins rattling into clean margarine tubs. And then the long summer evenings at our local, Ned's, after the games. Hogging the pool table, fifty-pence coins lined up on its edge. Playing endless games of Puzzle

Bobble on the arcade machine in the corner. Roaming the long elbow-shaped street of Moneygall, popping into Mossie's shop for bags of penny sweets.

I became adept at carrying many things at once: hurley tucked in the crook of my arm so that I could hold my tennis ball in one hand and my bottle of Coke in the other; penny sweets getting warm and pliant in my pocket.

It is hard to describe the hold that a sport like hurling has on a small community like Moneygall – unless you've lived it and grown up in the intensity of its gaze, in which case you only realize how unusual it is when you move away. Hurling dictated our lives. Every summer, my parents brought us on a week's holiday, on city breaks to Cork or Galway or Westport, staying in self-catering student apart-ments that were let out for the summer months. Dad, usually involved as a selector with one Moneygall team or another, would often leave us midweek to return home for a fixture, coming back late at night or early the next morn-ing. Even now, Dad is reluctant to go on holiday in the prime summer months, lest he miss a game, whether club or intercounty. Once my brother Conor began playing at senior level for Moneygall, the emotional stakes were amped up, and a loss or a poor team performance could result in a dark cloud descending on the house for days. I am continuing the cycle in my own small household, often being so on edge the morning of a game that my partner Cal refers to me as a 'bag of cats'. I'll enter a grieving period of perhaps two days if we lose – or worse, if I feel that I haven't performed to the best of my ability.

*

As a kid I knew that some families had more money than others, usually based on factors like whether my peers had TVs or PlayStations in their bedrooms; if they went abroad on holiday; what cars their parents drove. But class divisions in rural Ireland don't have quite the same force that they have in cities. There is often only one show in town: one school to go to, one pub to socialize in, one club to play for.

A Gaelic games hero is crowdsourced, raised and built by the village. Everyone in the community feels a connection to that person. Maybe you trained them when they were only under-10, and even then you could see their potential. Most likely your own kids played on the school or club team with them. Everyone feels ownership of local GAA heroes and also helps to keep them on the ground. 'There's no ego about him at all,' you'll often hear about a GAA star. 'Very low-key. Pure normal.' Ego – or even obvious self-esteem – is a cardinal sin in the GAA.

What I mean is, the making of a GAA hero happens in the full view of a community. There's no separate specialized training process like in horse-racing or gymnastics or sailing. It all occurs in the village's arena, the GAA pitch. From the time you're a child, you're held, supported, and scrutinized by your community.

There is fierce snobbery about hurling people too. We allow that athletes in other sports – boxing, say, or rowing – can take it up later in life, say in their mid-teens, and still achieve incredible results. Olympic medals, even, as in the cases of Kellie Harrington and Fintan McCarthy. Hurling is different, though; hurling is special. So the received wisdom goes. To achieve any sort of mastery, you need to be born with a hurl in your hand.

When I was ten, the Moneygall under-12 team got to a North final. I started at right-half forward. I played all right, but I hit a couple of wides and finished scoreless. We lost by a couple of points, and I bitterly regretted missing out on a hurling medal, which I already understood to be more real somehow than camogie medals. I had wanted to win not just for myself but for my dad. My personal disappointment was nothing to the disappointment that, in my ten-year-old brain, I imagined he was going through, though he would have been distressed to know that I felt that way.

I remember that final for another reason. It was especially hot that day, and we sat tightly packed in the dressing-room before the game. There were two other girls in the room besides me. One of the selectors came in to announce the team and toss the jerseys from the bag to each player as he called their name, a ritual I've always loved. The boys around me began to take off their t-shirts in anticipation of the jerseys, a row of shirtless lads bordering the room. I usually wore a vest under my t-shirt and thus under my jersey, but on that day I didn't. Like I said, it was hot.

I took off my t-shirt.

I don't remember anything being said, but it seemed to me that the atmosphere in the room changed instantly. The lads on the bench to either side of me moved away fractionally, as far as the packed dressing-room would allow. The selector could not meet my eye as he handed me my jersey. Seeking reassurance, I looked over to the two other girls, but they were busy performing a move that I would soon become adept at: simultaneously removing their t-shirts and getting into their jerseys while staying covered at all times.

This is my first memory of feeling deep shame about my body. That day I learned that while it was fine for a boy to be shirtless, if a girl did the same thing she was topless: exposed. From my perspective, we all looked the same: pale, skinny, flat-chested. But somehow, they were allowed this small liberty and I was not.

It was a line in the sand. Up until then, I hadn't really seen any difference between myself and the boys. I hadn't thought much about my own body at all. It wasn't that the hurley was an extension of my arm; I felt that I was an extension of the hurley. The hurling worked through me; I was the instrument, not it. We were all just hurlers.

3. Teenage Misfit

I kept playing on the hurling team until under-16 level, at which point I was noticeably shorter and lighter than most of the other players on the pitch, and no longer making the starting fifteen. Julie and I regularly togged out in whatever facilities there were for female patrons at the venues, breathing the smell of ammonia from the seldom-cleaned toilets, feeling the cold of the concrete floor under our bare feet as we balanced on one leg, pulling on our hurling socks while standing up.

It was thrilling, though, to be able to hold my own against the boys while I could. I remember being stuck in corner-forward in an under-12 match against Nenagh, becoming increasingly frustrated that the ball wasn't coming my way. And then a ball did come my way. I was second to it, again; my man gathered it and turned to strike. Holding the hurley short, I went to block him, and somehow my thumb got trapped between the two hurleys. I looked down at my thumbnail: already, it was turning black.

You can't go down. Not as one of a handful of girls on a pitch full of boys. You can never show weakness, never give them a reason to say you don't belong there. You keep playing, even as you become dizzy with the pain.

Eventually, the ball came into the corner and I was able to scramble to it first. I ran along the endline and angled it into the goal, the euphoria of scoring momentarily short-circuiting the pain. Not long after, I was taken off.

The next twenty-four hours were difficult, the blood continuing to swell beneath the thumbnail, creating a painful pressure. I went to my doctor, who sterilized a needle and burnt a hole in the nail, releasing the blood and alleviating the pressure. The keratin eventually patched over, but for a while, every time I looked down and saw the hole in my thumbnail, I thought of that goal and smiled. It looked for all the world like a ball hitting the back of the net.

Summer camps were an exciting prospect, a chance to play hurling for hours in the sun, to show people what you were made of. There were skills competitions, free t-shirts. Sometimes someone from a bordering parish would parachute in, and it was fun to play against new people, whose style of play you weren't familiar with.

While nearly all the boys I played alongside treated me as a teammate, there were the odd few who were confused by and resentful of my presence. I remember once a tall boy named Tomás, a few years older than me, of limited hurling skill but accustomed to dominating through his size. I marked him on the first day of camp, scoring a couple of points, and he never forgave me for it, doing his best to undermine and exclude me for the rest of the week. Once, when we were on the same team and I scored a point, he berated me for it.

'We need a goal. What a waste. You're selfish with the ball, that's your problem.'

He wasn't like this with anyone else, and I surmised that

there were no good girl hurlers where he was from, and he didn't know what to make of me.

The lads on my team for the most part protected me. I remember our centre-back, Sean, getting in a lad's face for calling me a bitch on the field. And I remember my cousin Eoghan quietly taking me to one side one day at training and showing me how to take a sideline cut. As a wing-forward, I was often the nearest player to this particular set-piece, and I hadn't been setting the world alight. Rather than give out to me, Eoghan helped.

'You're holding the hurley too loosely,' he said – and I was. I loved the ritual of the sideline: placing the ball, stepping back, the approach and the shape it made. I'd been giving myself an indulgent wrist rotation and elaborate swing of the hurley before genuflecting to the ball, aping the lads on telly. 'You need to grip it tight,' Eoghan said.

I tried it his way, and it worked. Even now, when I step up to a sideline – whether in training or in the thick of a match – I say those words in my mind.

I was lucky that Moneygall camogie club was founded in 1995, 110 years after the earliest iteration of Moneygall hurling club. It gave me a safe place to land, once hurling with the lads was no longer viable. All of us felt an owner-ship of the club: it felt good to step into something with no history, to build something from scratch.

At the tail-end of the nineties, I began secondary school in Roscrea. The three schools in the town – the Christian Brothers, the convent, and the vocational school or 'tech' – were in the process of amalgamating into a community college on the campus of the old tech. For a few years the student body wore a mishmash of uniforms – Brothers' grey, convent blue, tech navy and community college black – separating us into visibly demarcated factions.

I began playing camogie under the guidance of the laconic and droll English teacher Emmet Arrigan, who wore green Hunter wellies on the muddy school pitch. (I was slightly in awe of him, in part because he was married to Mary Arrigan, one of my favourite children's authors.) Despite Mr Arrigan's genuine interest, and the tech's strong hurling identity, there was not a big camogie culture within the school. Once, our entire year got a half-day to go support the lads' team, but I had to personally excuse myself to my teachers if I had to leave early for camogie. It was the type of school where the popular girls would flock to school hurling games to support their boyfriends, and mutter 'State of her, she's such a man' as I walked past them in the corridor with my hurley and gearbag.

Almost immediately in secondary school I was at sea. I no longer understood how anything worked socially. What I knew about adolescence I'd learned from observing my sister Eileen. From her, I knew that being a teenager involved shopping, sleepovers, waitressing in the summers, and occasionally heading off to the Gaeltacht for a couple of weeks. She'd inducted me into *Tragic Kingdom*, *Jagged Little Pill* and *Friends*; she let me read her old copies of *J-17*, which distilled adolescence into boy bands, horoscopes and snogging tips. The life of a teen seemed glamorous, but I had no idea how I was supposed to step into that role and inhabit it.

In primary school, you won respect by being able to jump off the biggest tomb in the Church of Ireland graveyard; on the hurling pitch, you won respect by being faster and more skilful and more relentless than the person next to you. Secondary school was a culture shock. Tomboys were no longer considered cute; when I tried to compete with the lads in badminton or in the co-ed soccer we sometimes played in PE, I received 'who does she think she is' eye rolls. You were not supposed to compete. You were supposed to observe. You were supposed to be adorably, flirtily uncoordinated, and allow the boys to show you how it's done. Instead, I wanted to destroy them.

I was bullied. I mention this because while it's an incredibly common experience, it is also something that shapes you irrevocably. After years of keeping my head down, trying not to be noticed, I still have trouble making eye contact with people. 'I am always surprised when people like me,' I found myself telling a therapist years later, a statement so bald and pathetic that I immediately wanted to stuff the words back inside my mouth.

It was the usual things. Exclusion. Dismissive laughter. Being mocked within earshot. Being talked about as if I was not there. Notes written about me where it was known I would find them. *Nobody likes Eimear,* read one. *She is a scab.* Being shouted at on the street. A couple of times, being shoved and threatened.

I didn't do much about it. My parents knew something was wrong but I clammed up when they tried to draw me out, unwilling to relive the humiliation by relating it. I didn't tell any teachers, because bullying was endemic in the school and I was aware that there were students who had it far worse than I did. Even some of the bullies had it worse than me: I was from a stable, supportive, middle-class

47

family and many of my classmates were not so lucky. Bullying me was perhaps a way of offsetting their own powerlessness; looking back, it's an understandable response to the stressors they were under. But to my eternal regret, I didn't stand up for myself: initially because I was so confused at what was happening, and later because I just hoped that if I didn't react, they'd get bored and leave me alone.

I began to fear large groups of girls. I began to fear settings that could not be quickly exited, such as buses. I was bullied in so many contexts and by so many different groups that I began to believe that it wasn't their problem, but mine. I carried myself as if trying to disappear. Everywhere except on the camogie pitch.

I don't know what I would have done if not for sport; if not for that chance to hurt and be hurt, to dominate the person nearest you, to pour all that anger and shame into hitting the ball as hard as you could. When I didn't have training or a match, I would go to the ball wall to expend energy, to not think about anything else for a while other than stick and ball and rebound. The simple quick mechanics of it. Even now, when I'm feeling low or frustrated, I pick up my hurley and ball and go outside. Sometimes it helps to remind yourself that you're good at something.

Like so many teenage outcasts before me, I took refuge in pop culture. The cruel things said to me in school played on a loop in my head, and the only way to quiet them was to disappear into music, TV shows, books and the internet.

The boy bands that had been my staple musical diet up

until my early teens were no longer fit for purpose; they didn't have the lyrical depth to help me through difficult moments. I distinctly remember bursting into tears on first listen of Five's 'Keep On Movin'' because the chorus's exhortation to 'get on up when you're down' seemed so trite and useless. (Oh Scott, if only it were that simple!) Increasingly I listened to stadium rock and – it being the noughties – nu-metal, whose anger and melancholy felt less alienating than the aggressive cheeriness of the charts.

The internet became both community and creative outlet: a way of finding other fans of the things I loved, of discussing and debating with them, of learning how to argue and analyse. I began reading, writing and posting fanfiction, and quickly became swept up in that world. You'd get instant feedback, both positive and negative, and because you were working in an established fictional world with beloved characters, there was no pressure to create – only to augment the established canon, like a paint-by-numbers set. It was an ideal sandbox for a burgeoning writer.

Things got better. I eventually found a scrappy group of fellow misfits – sweet-natured, creative girls and boys who loved talking about pop culture as much as I did. Some of them played sports, and if they thought me strange for committing to camogie to the extent that I did, they generally didn't tease me about it. We were all outcasts to an extent, had all been scuffed and bruised a little on the gravel path of adolescence. Trauma – even on a small scale – has a bonding effect. And we shared things. Well-thumbed Agatha Christies and Point Horrors, and later Chuck Palahniuks and Bret Easton Ellises; burned CDRs of White Stripes and Pixies albums; VHS tapes of *X-Files* and *Buffy* episodes recorded off Sky.

Pop culture gave me refuge, but it also cut me off. I developed an anxiety about being away from my books and my dial-up connection and my CDs and videos for extended periods. It was more than introversion. My head was almost always in the clouds. And I was unable to overcome my distrust of groups of girls – which was a barrier, obviously, in a camogie dressing-room.

The thing is, people in the world of sport generally have good self-esteem. They stand tall. They look you in the eye. They live in the moment. They talk about their families, their relationships, their part-time jobs and travel plans. Their actual lives. I wanted to talk about the use of uilleann pipes on Neutral Milk Hotel's *In the Aeroplane Over the Sea*, or what was the best cinematic adaptation of *Hamlet*, or at what point *Frasier* began to jump the shark. It seemed to me that I cared too much about the wrong things, and I still wonder if that is the condition and function of being a writer – dwelling too hard on minutiae so that the rest of society can focus on the big picture. It's not that my teammates didn't read books or enjoy movies or love music: of course they did. They just didn't proffer these things as a stand-in for a personality.

I try to have compassion for myself, looking back. My sense of self had been dismantled and, like countless others before me, I tried to reconstruct it using pop culture as my primary materials. I became incapable of being vulnerable or authentic. All I would show people was this refracted mosaic of things that meant something to me. Unable to offer my real self, instead I would say: I like this thing. Maybe you will like it too?

The writer George Saunders has an exercise about artistic influences that he says always 'lit up the room' when he deployed it with a group of students. You take a sheet of paper and make a grid. On the x-axis you put age ranges: 0–5, 5–10, 10–15, 15–20, and so on until your current age bracket. On the y-axis you put pop cultural categories: books, music, movies, TV, video games, toys, etc. Then you fill it in – honestly, not aspirationally.

'The focus here is on emotional engagement,' Saunders writes. 'What did you obsessively watch? What book did you read until the cover fell off? What story were you always fantasizing yourself into?'

Saunders's point is that while writers may say – or may, on some level, wish – that their influences are Chekhov or Joyce or Borges or Woolf, our influences are often much more humble and lowbrow; or at least, we have to love a lot of lowbrow properties before we're in a position to love highbrow ones. But his point is also that the development of a writer begins early. 'A person becomes an artist in that moment she or he recognizes that art has power,' he writes. 'Sensing that power, we want to participate – we want to learn how to be powerful in that way.'

Creative people don't just enjoy stories as a way to pass the time, before turning back to the more important project of life: they are obsessive. They want to climb into stories, live in them, pull them apart to see how they work – and they know from a young age that they want to spend their life doing that. It becomes their entire identity, they can't shut up about it, and it occasionally makes them insufferable to be around.

Looking at my own grid, I see the TV shows that made me want to create and that provided safe havens from humiliation and fear. I see the music that gave me grist and motivation both on and off the pitch. I see the movies that transported me far away from rural Ireland, reassuring me that there were other places and ways to be. And I see the writers who I wanted to become, who I read over and over as if I could replace the voices in my head with theirs.

Years later, in my mid-twenties, I ended up talking to one of my former antagonists in a bar one night. She had bullied me when we were in our early teens. Then there had been a few years of uneasy peace. We kept crossing paths, and as we both grew up I began to genuinely like her; she became gentler, less cutting, more sure of herself. On the night in question, we were reminiscing. I made a self-deprecating reference to being picked on as a kid before I'd even processed who I was talking to.

'Were you?' she asked.

'Well, yeah,' I said. 'I mean, I was a bit of a weirdo.'

She smiled. 'I never thought that about you.'

Probably, she was just being polite. Maybe she wanted to smooth over a slightly awkward bump in the conversation. But in that moment, I considered the terrifying possibility that my bullies, who changed the way I interacted with the world and altered my personality forever, simply did not remember the way they had treated me. It had never been about me at all.

4. Senior Hurling

When I was seventeen, before I realized that it was impossible to write about sports without sounding hyperbolic or hopelessly romantic, I wrote a novel about camogie. I wanted to be a writer and, being a fairly sheltered and well-behaved teenager from the midlands, camogie was the only life experience I had to work with.

The draft has survived down the years on the external hard drive that I use to transfer files when one laptop expires and a new one is acquired. It was last modified on August 31st, 2006: abandoned at 37,000 words, the mid-novel hump. There's a frantic, excitable feel to the text, of the sort that only a teenage girl can produce, and helpful expository digressions at the start of each chapter for those not indoctrinated into the sport from birth. *Come into my gaah world*, the novel pleads on every page. *See how cool it is? See how hardcore we are?*

I was called up to the Tipperary senior camogie panel in early 2004 at the same time as my friend and clubmate Julie Kirwan. Both of us had recently turned seventeen, and had played together on countless teams since we were children: under-12, under-14 and under-16 with the Moneygall hurlers; under-14, minor, junior, intermediate and senior with Moneygall camogie club; schools camogie with Coláiste Phobal Roscrea; and under-14,

minor and intermediate with Tipperary. Julie was a tena-
cious, attacking defender who organized our backline
with ease and confidence; I was our freetaker and primary scorer. We were two sides of a coin, and had shared
every accolade in our careers. It made sense that we were
called up together.

Along with Joanne Nolan of Silvermines, a versatile
and stylish player who was drafted in as a sub goalie, we
were the youngest members of the panel. I was half in
awe of the veterans of the team, who were as close to
household names as camogie players got – Ciara Gaynor,
Deirdre Hughes, Eimear McDonnell, Therese Brophy,
Una O'Dwyer and Jovita Delaney – and of our charis-
matic manager, former Tipp wing-back Raymie Ryan.

My expectations, as a new member of a successful
county panel, were great. Having won their very first All-
Ireland in 1999, Tipperary had won four out of the last
five. I felt that it would always be this way. More than that,
I would be a lynchpin of the next generation of players, a
wing-forward on the next All Ireland-winning team, perhaps. None of these things came about. Tipp hasn't won
an All-Ireland in almost two decades, and I never broke
into the first fifteen.

It being 2004, the squad was awash with money. People
were lining up to sponsor us. About a month after I first
started training with them, the entire 2003 panel headed
off to the States to celebrate the previous year's All-Ireland
win. Expenses were generous. 'Do you need a new pair of
boots?' Raymie would ask us. 'Any physio sessions? A few
spare hurleys?' The sport being, technically, amateur, there
was often nowhere for the money to go other than to buy

us all a new kit for every championship game. For a time there, I could have outfitted my own seven-a-side team in Tipperary hoodies, socks, skorts – that mystical union of skirt and shorts – and those ubiquitous O'Neill's navy tracksuit bottoms. Once I stopped training with the Tipp squad, I never wore those tracksuit bottoms again. Even now, whenever I hear the swish of somebody walking past in them, I am transported back to those dressing-rooms, those fields.

2004 was the centenary of the Camogie Association, and rumours swirled that the All-Ireland camogie final would be the curtain-raiser for the hurling final, a slot usually given to the minor hurlers.

This is major, goes the tagline for the All-Ireland minor championships. In its cinematic and beautifully shot TV ad, the heroes are tall and good-looking lads, on their way to being men. The scrawny red-headed kid gets picked last. Girls appear in flashes, slow-dancing with the hero or sitting in rows on the field's perimeter wall. Watching the lads from the sidelines.

The idea of the double-header seemed so obvious and sensible that I wondered why it didn't happen every year. Camogie finals pull in a respectable crowd of 15–20,000, but in the vastness of Croke Park, that number can feel sparse. Didn't the players – and the sport as a whole – deserve the spotlight, the full glare of 80,000 spectators? It bothered me greatly that more prominence was afforded to minor lads than to senior women.

I'm not sure why it didn't happen, in the end. Some say that it was the decision of the Camogie Association, preferring to have their own day out, too proud to play second fiddle. In any case, it strikes me as a missed opportunity. Women's sports that are staged alongside their male counterparts – track and field, tennis, swimming – draw comparable levels of interest and attention. When you treat men and women as if they are playing the same sport – which, of course, they are – you get something close to equality of esteem. It helps if, as in the case of the above sports, you have a single governing body looking after both sexes, nationally and internationally.

Gaelic games have not one but three administrative structures: the Gaelic Athletic Association (founded 1884), the Camogie Association (founded 1904) and the Ladies Gaelic Football Association (founded 1974). One might think that there's potential here for independence and innovation on the part of the Camogie Association and LGFA, but in practice the situation has been disastrous for female players. It's especially hard on those who play both camogie and ladies' football: the two women's organizations seem not to consult one another when making fixture calendars, and dual players frequently find themselves double-booked at both club and county level. In contrast, the GAA – which governs both hurling and men's Gaelic football – coordinates its fixtures to ensure that there are no clashes between its two major codes, making the life of a dual player workable, if unavoidably challenging.

When the GAA was founded in 1884, it made no provision for female players. The historian Paul Rouse spoke eloquently on the subject for the hurling documentary series *The Game*. 'The place of women within hurling', he said, was 'absolutely reflective of the place of women in Irish society'. The idea that women might actually play the game 'doesn't seem to have dawned on anyone'.

In 2017, the poet Ailbhe Ní Ghearbhuigh began writing an article for an academic journal about the roots of camogie. Ailbhe and I had bonded over our mutual love of feminist podcasts and Maggie Nelson. She ended up writing about camogie almost by accident.

'What can you tell me about Cáit Ní Dhonnchadha?' she asked me. The name meant nothing to me. Ailbhe told me that Cáit was a young Gaelic activist who, along with her brother, Tadhg, and the association's first president, Máire Ní Chinnéide, founded the Camogie Association in 1904 – twenty years after the GAA was founded as an organization in which only boys and men would appear on the field of play. Even amidst the Camogie Association's centenary celebrations in 2004, I don't remember ever hearing the founders' names.

Ailbhe came across Cáit during her postdoctoral research, as she sifted through the papers of Cáit's brother, Tadhg Ó Donnchadha, in the Boole Library at University College Cork. Tadhg – or Torna, the pen-name by which he was more widely known – was a raffish-looking fellow with a long, waxed moustache. He was a Professor of Irish at UCC, a prominent member of the Gaelic League and the GAA, and by far the more famous of the two siblings. He was influential in the formalizing of camogie, drawing up the rules and coining its name. Ailbhe found a scrapbook of Cáit's as an unlisted item among Torna's papers. Until then, she hadn't known Cáit existed, and neither had I.

*

2004 ended up being one of the most condensed and scheduled years of my life. I began training three times a week with the Tipp senior team – Tuesdays, Thursdays and Sunday mornings – and was also studying for my Leaving Cert. On the weekdays that we trained, I would get up at 6 a.m. to get in two hours of study before school. The year passed in a blur, and even now, nineteen years later, I struggle to situate myself in it.

We trained at Dr Morris Park in Thurles, next to Semple Stadium, where the Tipperary hurlers also trained. Raymie's sessions were fast and sharp, at a higher tempo than I'd ever played before. We were told to run at the ball full-pace and take it at speed; I missed it over and over before finally adapting. We were told to put our hands to the sliotar whenever possible, to ping the ball to each other at head-height.

Julie excelled: almost immediately, she made the first fifteen, and held that position through the league, Munster and All-Ireland campaigns. I, by contrast, got just a couple of runs throughout the year. I started a game against Dublin in the league at right-half forward and scored a point, which merited me a mention in the paper – a thrill to me both as a player and an aspiring journalist. I came on at midfield in the latter stages of a championship match against Wexford in which we were well ahead, and marked the great Kate Kelly, which even in the moment felt like an honour. I played in Semple Stadium, and though the place was mostly empty it still felt heightened, as if the trace of old clashes remained in the ground.

We got all the way to the All-Ireland final. It was Tipp's third final in a row against Cork; Tipp had lost in 2002 and won in 2003. I remember being stunned at the beauty and spaciousness of the Croke Park dressing-rooms, at the warmup area with its ball wall and astroturf. I remember Raymie shouting his pre-match pep talk, the one time all year I saw him lose his cool. I remember Deirdre Hughes banging in two goals: we had more stylish forwards than Dee, but none more clever, reliable or ruthless. I remember our captain, Joanne Ryan, lifting the cup. I had spent the match trying to keep my emotions, which were pin-balling all over the place, vaguely presentable. I'd wanted desperately to get the nod from management and have that waking-dream moment of running out on the pitch, while knowing deep down it was a long shot, and trying to be okay with that fact. I wanted to be overjoyed at the win for the sake of the team, but I felt unable to bury my personal disappointment. It was exhausting, and I hadn't even pucked a ball.

We watched *The Sunday Game* that night over dinner at the Skylon Hotel in Drumcondra, and on videotape the next day at lunchtime. There was no dressing up for the All-Ireland dinner, not in those days; we wore our Tipp polo shirts and zipper-cuff tracksuit bottoms. It was surreal to be the subject of *The Sunday Game*, a show we'd all grown up with, its theme tune imprinted on our consciousness. There was, at the same time, a slight disappointment: this wasn't the regular *Sunday Game* with Cyril and Tomás, but a special edition with former camogie players who were given a pundit gig once a year. While we understood what they were trying to do, it was a record-scratch all the same. We didn't want female refs or female pundits – we wanted the best, or what we perceived as the best, and at the time that usually meant men. (By now, thankfully, *The Sunday Game* has a number of excellent female pundits in its regular lineup.)

I remember that night in the Skylon's bathroom, after far too many pint bottles of cider, being coached by teammates on the best methods of throwing up. I remember the bus home, stopping off in the Poitín Stil for slabs of cans, the panel's mix CD (which was, for some reason, Bonnie Tyler-heavy) playing over the speaker system as we danced in the aisles.

The next day, the Monday, I turned eighteen. I was due to begin studying journalism at DCU, but first we had the homecoming in the Ragg, the village outside Thurles where the county camogie grounds are situated. As we cheered and waved to the crowd on an open-top bus, I thought to myself, *I don't deserve this.* The feeling of terrible unearned power followed me through several subsequent functions and school visits. I was told I was a role model and asked to give speeches. I presented medals. I was given lumps of crystal and bronze by various organizations. I received congratulatory cards from local politicians. I walked into my old secondary school gym as 'We Are the Champions' blared through the speakers. I climbed on stage to make a speech and looked down at the crowd – friends, classmates, neighbours and teachers, but also the girls who bullied me, the boys who never spoke to me. They were clapping and cheering now. I felt at the time that I hadn't earned any of it, and that feeling has never left me.

I didn't gel socially with the group any more than I excelled on the pitch. This was not for lack of trying on my part, nor is it an indictment of the panel who were, to a player, open and welcoming and friendly. But it's easy to spot the introvert in a group of self-assured, gregarious sports-women. On team buses, I would bring a book and a minidisc player to insulate myself. I liked talking to my teammates on a one-to-one basis, but I struggled with the group dynamics, the collective craic.

The camogie dressing-room can be a lonely place. It has a bristling, tense atmosphere: a peculiar mix of jockish bravado, slagging, and reticent Irish female modesty. The jangle of multiple female voices like so many bracelets on an arm; the short sharp shocks of laughter. My current dressing-room is full of brilliant, kind and hilarious women, but I'm still not fully at ease there.

There was also the undeniable fact that I was still a nerd. I listened to the music of whispery Christians like Sufjan Stevens and Belle & Sebastian and thought – in my adoles-cent way – that this made me intellectual and deep. I loved *Buffy* and *Star Wars* and *Harry Potter* and received blank stares when I tried to talk to my teammates about them.

It is only now, looking back, that I realize I was drawn to pop cultural narratives in which an object or weapon is central to the protagonist's power. In *Harry Potter*, the semi-sentient wands choose their witch or wizard, and magic is almost impossible without them. In *Star Wars*, lightsabers carry huge emotional weight and a sense of identity, from Luke Skywalker's – inherited from his father via Obi-Wan Kenobi – to Darth Maul's double-ended hay-maker. Even Buffy has Mr Pointy, a favoured stake given to her by Kendra, another vampire slayer. I became fixated with a moment in the pilot episode of *Buffy* when she pulls a large chest out of her closet and removes its top layer to reveal a secret stash of stakes, bottles of holy water, crucifixes and garlic. It made me think of my gearbag in the bottom of my wardrobe, with its own arsenal of boots, helmet, socks and insulating tape. I rewound and rewatched the scene on my VHS boxset over and over without really knowing why. But that is what sport gives us: a chance to participate in the mythical framework that we all grow up hearing about, whether in legend or pop culture. You get weapons, training, comrades, banquets, days of victory and days of defeat. We can be heroes.

Like me, Buffy had an extracurricular activity involving wooden sticks that interfered with her social life and left her battered and bruised. Like me, she lived on the Hellmouth – though at least Buffy's was in Sunny California, rather than the Irish midlands. Like me, she carried the burden of a 'sacred duty' that couldn't easily be set aside. Like me, she often felt overwhelmed trying to keep all the compartmentalized aspects of her life ticking over. Unlike me, she did it all with ready quips and a superb fashion sense.

The Tipp training schedule became arduous: getting a bus from the DCU campus to the centre of Dublin, then a Luas from Middle Abbey Street to the Red Cow, then a lift to Thurles, two midweek nights and then again at the weekend. I would arrive back on campus close to midnight, exhausted and sore, and miss my 9 a.m. lectures the next day. I resented how training took me away from study, my tentative group of friends, the city.

After winning two out of two All-Irelands as manager,

Raymie sensibly quit and was replaced by Paddy McCor-
mack, an affable man who had enjoyed some success with
the Tipperary minor hurlers. It was clear from early on
that Paddy didn't much rate me as a player. *You need to work
on your left side*, I remember him telling me early on. *You
always favour your right.* I don't remember how I responded.
Did I tell him that my left was actually my stronger side,
the side I'd learned on, the side on which I hit frees? Or
was I so taken aback and mortified I simply nodded and
retreated?

At some point I lost patience and started ringing
Paddy up, badgering him for a chance: a run in a practice
match; to be played in the forwards, the only position I
knew, in our internal A-team versus B-team games. (I
was usually put midfield, the grammar of which I didn't
understand; I ran haplessly in the seemingly infinite
space.) I was desperate to make him see what I could do.
He was a nice man; he placated me. Always the unspoken
question: *Am I even needed on this squad? Why am I even here?*
He gave me time, he listened, and I felt that he did care
about me as a person – he spoke to me at length, for
example, about my burgeoning journalism career with
the *Nenagh Guardian*. But his mind was made up about
me as a player.

'You're not really a scorer, Eimear, are you?' he said
once, in cajoling tones. His tone was warm and invited
confidence, as if to say *come on, now.*

This cut me to the quick. If I had an identity as a hurler –
if you'd asked me what I did for my club, what my function
was – I would have said: I score. But he said it to me as if
this was an open secret or private joke, something we both

knew but had heretofore left unsaid. If I wasn't a scorer, what was I?

Ailbhe's research revealed that Cáit Ní Dhonnchadha was an important intermediary between the worlds of camogie, the Irish language revival, the co-operative movement and the theatre. She wrote many articles in Patrick Pearse's newspaper *An Claidheamh Soluis* and publicly debated the issues of the day in its pages. She even literally portrayed Ireland, Cathleen Ní Houlihan style, in the Language Procession, a parade through Dublin organized in 1909 to raise money for the National Language Fund.

Despite all this activity, she never found paid work and for most of her life was Torna's housekeeper. She lamented the sidelining of women in the Gaelic League, and viewed camogie as a vehicle through which Irishwomen could express self-confidence and self-sufficiency.

Ailbhe's article, published in the academic journal *Comhar Taighde*, compares Cáit to Mary Lamb or Dorothy Wordsworth, talented women in their own right who have been consigned by history to the role of sidekicks to their more famous brothers. Ailbhe notes other similarities between Cáit, Mary and Dorothy: they all suffered from mental illness, and none of them ever married.

If the dressing-room can be a lonely place, the dugout can feel desolate – particularly when you know, in your heart of hearts, that you're there permanently. Managers love to talk about how hurling is a squad game nowadays; certain players who start will be spent after forty minutes and often all five subs will be used. Fresh legs are always needed to close the game out. But that doesn't mean that subs 16 to 30 all feel equally vital and indispensable; there's a hierarchy here too. It's one thing to know that you'll more than likely be called on to do a specific job for the last twenty minutes of a game; it's quite another to know that you've no chance of a run.

Permanent status as a substitute brings out the same symptoms as unrequited love: jealousy, paranoia and yearning. You're forced to watch, stranded on the sidelines, as the game goes on without you. We all want to be active participants. We all want a role in the narrative, and the sense of powerlessness can be paralysing.

The lack of game time changed the nature of training for me. Training is supposed to be an opportunity to work on your skills, maintain fitness, and build understanding and trust with your teammates; it's supposed to be enjoyable. For me, it warped into a weird, pressurized sort of test. Every mistake – every fumbled ball or missed shot – was confirmation that I didn't belong there. Every small flourish of skill or deft touch, if unseen, hardly seemed to matter. If I did something good in front of my coach and it went unremarked on, did it even occur?

Managers' belief, and who they choose to believe in, is incredibly influential. It's a self-fulfilling prophecy. The player that is nurtured on the big stage grows in confidence, which feeds and enhances their performance. The player who is consistently excluded from teamsheets is tormented: confidence shot, questioning everything, frustrated with management but also with themselves. *Why can't I be what they want me to be?* You suspect you're going mad, but you're also eighteen, so that's par for the course.

I don't think I could ever be a manager, though since I started working as a literary editor I find I have more empathy for their position – or at least more understanding of bias and personal taste. I frequently reject work that I recognize as well-written but which does not excite me; it's simply *not for me.* This is the great privilege of being an editor. You're not just there to be an objective arbiter of good writing; you're there to pick your favourites, to go with your gut. A manager may recognize that a player has ability and also simply not like them as a player; both of these things can be true at the same time. Not everyone can be published and not everyone can play.

The comparison falls down at a certain point. The rejected writer can always bring their work to another editor, another publisher. The GAA player is stuck with their club and county of origin. Either you tough it out, wait for the manager in question to leave, or you give up.

I challenged Paddy again after our second consecutive All-Ireland final defeat in 2006, buoyed by Dutch courage. *You never gave me a run, Paddy.* In the last training session before the All-Ireland, I'd been at full-forward for a change, and had scored three points off the great Una O'Dwyer. *That was the first time I saw real potential in you,* he said. He had been training me for two years; I was nineteen and burned out. Paddy wouldn't return to the panel the following year, and neither would I.

A cold hurler is no use to anyone, my father used to tell me, stressing the importance of warmups. The same can be said for an unhappy hurler, but there's no quick fix for that.

My family told me to hang in there, that I was doing well to even be on the panel, that not everything happens instantly; to persevere. Looking back now, half a lifetime and several injuries later, I don't know why I didn't. I was at the peak of my fitness, pace and ability. I was in the top thirty camogie players in the county, a privilege and an honour that I wish I had appreciated more. It seems ludicrous now that I felt like a failure for not making it by the age of twenty. But it was my first big test. Everything had come easily to me until then; I didn't know how to engage with adversity, to wrestle with it, to enjoy it even. That came much later.

The loneliness of the unused panel member is heightened by the fact that it's so hard to express. In an environment focused on positivity and the collective good, no one wants to hear it. It's dispiriting, it's self-centred, it's covetous – and yet it's also entirely natural. How do panel members remain buoyant and motivated when they are well down the subs list, sometimes year after year?

Unused subs generally don't get interviewed. But in 2010 I came across an *Irish Independent* interview with Brian Dowling, who was called up to the Kilkenny senior hurling panel in 2002 at the age of nineteen. He had a promising debut season, scoring from play when he was brought on in the league final and Leinster final, but he broke his ankle in the summer of 2003 and struggled to come back from it. Brian Cody released him from the panel in the spring of 2004, around the time I was training my first sessions with Tipp.

When I first came across this interview I found it incredibly moving. In telling his own story, Dowling (who is now the All-Ireland winning Kilkenny camogie manager) was speaking to my experience, and that of countless others. 'It was [my] first big experience at county level and getting two points in a league final is probably something I will always remember but to be honest it is something I don't really like talking about now. I did it when I was 19 and it was disappointing I did not do too much for Kilkenny after that . . . It was devastating at the time. Like, I was on the panel when I was 18 and to be going at the age of 20, it was not nice . . . I probably didn't deal with it great because like most hurlers you are a confidence player and I would have taken it to heart. I was involved with the [All Ireland-winning] under-21s that year and probably didn't enjoy it as much as I should have enjoyed it. And maybe I was trying too hard to get back on the senior panel.'

When I look back, my biggest regret is my own lack of generosity – towards my teammates and towards myself. I did not recognize at the time that Julie's achievement in making the first fifteen was exceptional; in my head, it was the expected standard that I had failed to reach. Instead of treating my clubmate's success as inspiration, I used it as a stick to beat myself. I wasn't the only one to play into this narrative. 'Where's *your* All-Star?' a friend of my father's asked me the morning after the awards ceremony at which Julie was honoured. All in banter, of course. I had severe *esprit de l'escalier* for weeks later, wishing I had responded 'Same place as yours.'

There is a photo of me and the O'Duffy Cup framed on the dresser at home. I'm wearing a light-blue Tipperary tracksuit top and lifting it one-handed, posing for my mother's camera. In my right hand is my hurley and hel-met, unused. In all the excitement on the pitch, I'd gotten briefly separated from the rest of the squad, and was one of the last members of the panel to climb the steps of the Hogan and lift the cup.

In the top right-hand corner of the photo is my younger cousin Mary Ryan, face painted blue and gold, watching me and cheering. Mary would join the panel the following season – 2005 – and, within a few years, establish a place for herself in the Tipperary starting backline. Her career would be long and illustrious. She served as captain for several years and won an All-Star in 2020. She was a key figure in rebuilding the county team in the lean years post-2006; Tipp would not feature in an All-Ireland semi-final again until 2018, but would make the top four consistently for the next four years. She was a leader off the pitch as well, helping establish the Women's Gaelic Players' Asso-ciation in 2015. At the time of writing she has given eighteen years of her life to Tipperary camogie. She doesn't have an All-Ireland medal. Now, when I look at that pic-ture, I can't help but mentally reverse our positions: Mary lifting the cup, and me cheering her on.

One thing I've learned: talent is commonplace. Mental strength and maturity are rarer, and are ultimately what separate those that make it from those that don't. I was talented and technically proficient, but I was light, not par-ticularly fast, and tentative in the air. I needed nurturing, as all young players stepping up to the big stage do. But a county panel is a large and diverse entity with multiple needs and requirements, and when you're trying to win All-Irelands, the development of young players who *might* be ready a few years down the line is, understandably, not a priority.

There are bright spots, of course. I won't forget the kindness of Deirdre Hughes and Noelle Kennedy, giving us lifts to training before we had our own licences, endlessly spinning Dido's *Life for Rent* in the car. I won't forget Deirdre McDonnell's patience, giving me lifts from Dublin, waiting for me even when I showed up late, and dropping me back to the DCU campus at eleven at night. I won't forget Raymie Ryan's training sessions and his ability to check in with every member of an unwieldy, multi-generational panel, or guest coach Davy Fitzgerald keeping us training for two-and-a-half hours, his roar when we did something right: 'Perfect, perfect!'

Cáit Ní Dhonnchadha ended her days in Our Lady's Asylum in Cork, an imposing Gothic building that overlooks the city from Sunday's Well. Closed as a psychiatric hospital in 1992, the building is now an apartment complex.

According to hospital records, Cáit was diagnosed with 'dementia' at the age of twenty-nine, but wasn't admitted to Our Lady's until 1944, just over a decade later. Torna seems to have tried to support Cáit at home for as long as possible. He himself died in 1949, and his funeral was attended by Éamon de Valera. Cáit lived another twenty years.

For a time, her final resting place wasn't publicly known. Her death notice gave no clues aside from 'private burial'. Ailbhe visited the grave of Torna and his wife in Glasheen Cemetery. The headstone bears both their names: Tadhg Ó Donnchadha and Nóra Ní Fhoghludha. It was only when

Ailbhe consulted the cemetery's records that she saw *Cáit Ní Dhonnchadha* listed under the same plot, uncredited even in death.

For a long time, I didn't know where my All-Ireland medal was. When I moved out of my parents' house in 2016 – finally, properly, taking all my childhood detritus with me – I brought with me a shoebox full of medals from various club, county and school competitions. I assumed the All-Ireland medal was in there somewhere, but when I dug through the box out of curiosity, I couldn't find it.

It showed up finally in an attic trawl, smaller and more charming than I remembered. A special centenary medal, it depicts those women of 1904, trailblazers like Cáit Ní Dhonnchadha, swinging their hurleys in ankle-length skirts. It is also, in a way that seems amusing and appropriate, slightly tarnished.

I showed it to my father, then asked him to show me his medals in return: the senior north and county medals that he earned with Moneygall. In 1975, the Moneygall hurlers did the double, winning both north and county titles, a feat unequalled before or since. In 1976, though beaten in the group stages in the north, they still qualified as one of sixteen teams to defend their county title, beating Roscrea by a single point in the final. The north medal portrays Tipperary patriot Thomas MacDonagh, while the two counties feature the old Tipperary crest. All three are gold.

Not literal gold, of course. Medals are as talismanic as religious objects, their value utterly contingent on how you feel about them. Depending on how you look at it, a medal can be just another trinket, or imbued with magic.

My dad had uncertain years with Tipperary, too. Hard years with St Flannan's of Ennis, where he went to school. In fairness, he tried to prepare me. Not everyone will value the sort of player you are. Not everyone will give you a chance. This is yet another way sport prepares you for life, lets you experience the sting of failure or exclusion in a relatively safe space.

That's the beauty of sport. The stakes are as low or as high as you want them to be. It can mean nothing, or everything. You get to decide.

5. East Coast

I togged out in my last Tipperary jersey just as I was entering my third year of college. What residual sporting energy I had, I put into the college team. DCU had never been a camogie stronghold, but a strong group of us – including several Dublin senior players – came together and something clicked. We won a Purcell Shield in my third year: a lesser trophy, but the first bit of camogie silverware the college had won in a while and a source of intense pride all the same.

It may also have been the first dressing-room where I fitted in, where I didn't feel I had to hide parts of myself, where I could talk about books, music and pop culture and not be met with blank stares or told I was taking things too seriously. This group played camogie first and foremost for the enjoyment – just like they drank for enjoyment and argued about Oscar contenders for enjoyment. It was the perfect antidote for the negative feelings I had stockpiled against the sport. I acquired a nickname – 'Ryaner', which would be impossible in a Tipperary context, for obvious reasons. I even enjoyed the bus journeys.

I was lucky enough during my time in DCU to be granted a sports scholarship for my first three years. The first year, it was an incredibly generous and valuable award – €1,000 directly into my bank account, plus a gym membership. The second year, it was €500 into the bank account, an additional €500 claimable through vouched expenses, and the gym. The third year it was vouched expenses and gym only. It would have been fine had us female GAA players not been dogged by stories of what the lads received: bursaries, free accommodation, substandard exam results that got over the line all the same. Probably some of this was apocryphal, but what was true was that Sigerson Cup was king at DCU, and the Sigerson lads were treated like royalty.

That third year, I bought a few hundred euros' worth of expensive sports gear, but didn't have the enthusiasm or will to put it to any good use. I rarely darkened the door of the gym; I let my free membership lapse. Mentally, I was already gone.

In January 2007, I was in a pub in Santry with my friend and classmate Claire Ryan, with whom I was completing a joint project. We had a habit of rewarding ourselves for the slightest bit of output with drinking sessions. (Claire now lives in Tokyo and is an accomplished marathon runner who drinks only the occasional beer.)

A phone call came through to my mobile from an unknown number. I knew from teammates that the new Tipperary management was making calls. I went outside to the beer garden, empty in winter but for a few hardy smokers. Would I be available for training? I hemmed and hawed. I told them I would have to think about it. I was tempted by the fresh start but fearful of repeating the same old story, the familiar sinking feeling of not making it. What if it wasn't that the management didn't get me – what if it was me? What if I just wasn't at the standard?

There was another, practical concern. In the first semester of my final year of college – that autumn – I would be heading abroad for a few months of study. Where, I wasn't yet sure, but I knew that if we made it to the All-Ireland final again – and there was no reason to believe we wouldn't – I would not be in the country. Was it worth committing for the year if I was going to miss the business end of championship?

Of course it is, said everyone – the new manager, my parents, my teammates. My friend Claire, however, said two magical words to me: *Just quit.* She said it like it was nothing, like it was easy. You are allowed to walk away from things that make you unhappy. You don't have to keep banging your head off the same wall. But I'd internalized so many of the core values of Gaelic games – service, honest effort, the sublimation of the ego and submission to the good of the team, never *ever* giving up – that it took three years of frustration, and my friend's magic words, before I grasped that this was an option.

So I quit – in retrospect, one of the first adult decisions I ever made. If my father was disappointed in my decision, he hid it well. He'd had his own unhappy experiences with teams. But my mother – a south Tipp woman by birth, who fully embraced the hurling way of life after moving to Moneygall – was uneasy about it. She hadn't raised a quitter.

That August I flew to Boston with three classmates for my semester abroad. After much deliberation I took my hurleys with me, packaged up tight and designated by the airline as 'Special Baggage'.

I had done my due diligence, emailing the only Boston camogie club I could find on the internet. I received a polite response from their secretary to say that, alas, their season ended in September so it would be hardly worth my while. Still, I was afraid on some level to be without the hurleys.

We subletted an unfurnished place in Allston where the walls were painted in alternating garish colours: orange, red, lime green. We ate off plastic plates and slept on inflatable mattresses for the duration of the semester because, we reasoned, it wasn't worth investing in proper dishes or bedding for four months.

We were to study at Boston University, perhaps the least famous of the city's big third-level institutions but still impressively grand: a string of buildings on the south bank of the Charles River. There was no distinction between the university and the surrounding city: Commonwealth Avenue ploughed right through the campus, with several T stops along the way.

There was a Barnes & Noble on campus with a full floor of BU merchandise; I bought a t-shirt and baseball cap in my first week, marking myself out as an over-enthusiastic newbie. We were supposed to be furthering our studies in journalism, but I spent my credits on introductory courses I wouldn't get a chance to do at home: psychology, Shakespeare and creative writing. The psychology class was at 8 a.m. and everyone made it, even when it snowed and the T stalled on the tracks. The creative writing class was held in one of the campus's oldest buildings, all turrets and staircases and small seminar rooms. On our first day of class, our tutor – a laid-back grad student named Maddie – told us that Sylvia Plath had once studied in these very rooms.

The grandeur of this statement settled on us a moment; we all looked at each other meaningfully. We would all write great things here – I mean, we would have to, to appease Sylvia's ghost. When, later, I tried to verify this – whether Sylvia Plath had actually studied at BU – I found out only that her mother had done her undergraduate degree there and her father had been a professor of biology there. Perhaps Sylvia took summer classes at BU, I'm not sure.

Since I was a child, I'd wanted two things: to be a professional hurler and a professional writer. The pro hurling wasn't going to work out – which was only partially my fault – and I could tell from three years of journalism that I wasn't really cut out to be a news reporter either, being a shy, anxious type. I had stopped writing fiction when I got to college, trying to re-orientate my writing towards the real, the newsworthy, the five Ws. Now I was far away from home and gave myself permission to try and fail.

Every week we gathered in that turreted room to read and write and dissect each other's work. Sometimes Maddie brought doughnuts. Sometimes she said my name phonetically, other times correctly. (I adopted the name Emma for my Starbucks orders.) Maddie had us read Tobias Wolff and Amy Hempel and Flannery O'Connor and Carlos Fuentes, stories that warped my brain in the best way, showing me what was possible. She called me out on my bullshit: 'You can't always just have the characters bone when you run out of story, Eye-mer.' But she was encouraging too, telling me that I had good instincts, encouraging me to apply for internships at local literary journals. I would have loved to, but I was due back in Ireland by Christmas.

I spent a great deal of my parents' money in bookstores. I read Rick Moody and Alice Munro and William Trevor and Miranda July and Karen Russell. The short story was a new and miraculous form to me. Unlike poetry, stories hadn't been dissected to death in school – they'd been pretty much ignored. We'd read Liam O'Flaherty's 'The Sniper' at some point, and Brendan Behan's 'The Confirmation Suit', and probably Frank O'Connor's 'Guests of the Nation', but despite all the talk of the great Irish short story, it didn't much feature in my education. In America, short stories felt vital, and books were published by young people under titles like *No One Belongs Here More Than You* and *Everything Here Is the Best Thing Ever*. They wrote about alligator-wrestling and inappropriate crushes and black magic rituals gone wrong. I thought of the stories I'd been writing for the workshop about middle-aged alcoholics in rural Ireland, at the end of which two characters might improbably bone, and resolved to do better.

I ignored the hurleys for a couple of months, leaving them in the corner of my sparsely furnished room, still in their plastic wrapping from the aeroplane hold. But I could not, it seemed, ignore sport. As soon as I was allowed set foot in a sports bar (I did not turn twenty-one until a month into my stay), I quickly became swept up in Red Sox fever. The Sox were on track to win their second World Series in four years; their previous victory, in 2004, had ended an eighty-six-year famine. The Curse of the Bambino had finally been broken. Having won the World Series in 1918, the Red Sox sold its star pitcher Babe Ruth to the New York Yankees in the off-season of 1919–20, thus beginning a golden era for the Yankees and a decades-long losing streak for the Red Sox. Coming from a GAA background, I had, of course, been reared on curses: Biddy Early's curse which kept Clare hurlers in the wilderness for eighty-odd years, and the Mayo curse of '51, yet to be broken. I found baseball confusing at first, but the curses I understood.

Over time, baseball came to entrance me in the same way that snooker did. It was boring to watch, and yet hypnotizing. At any given moment there was a slim chance that something might happen, and you could not look away in case you missed it; the whole enterprise rested on that tension. I went to Fenway Park with my siblings when they visited, a low-stakes game against the Los Angeles Angels. The Red Sox won 9–1, giving us plenty to cheer about. I bought a foam finger, which I regretfully had to leave behind me when I left Boston that December.

If you watched baseball, you could strike up a conversation with pretty much anyone in the city: your barista, your bookstore clerk, the guy in your creative writing class who always wore a baseball cap, even indoors in a humid September. It was social currency, even social survival. I was amazed at how quickly the players' names rooted themselves in my mind, as firmly as any Tipp hurlers that I'd idolized down the years. Even now I can conjure them in a commentator's drawl: Jason Varitek, Mike Lowell, Manny Ramirez, Dustin Pedroia, David Ortiz. My favourite was Diasuke Matsuzaka, a Japanese pitcher in his rookie year, whose name the Red Sox fans phoneticized to Dice-K. He was young and unflappable, and always seemed to be enjoying himself, even under ferocious pressure – a sporting attitude which I have always aspired to and never attained.

Drinking in sports bars, I would inevitably start trying to explain hurling to Americans. People would comment on my accent and ask where I was from, or would ask about the small silver hurley that I wore on a chain around my neck. My friend Paul could never remember how to say 'Tipperary'; he would forget the penultimate long midlands vowel, rhyme it with 'frippery' and make me crack up. He took me to a batting cage once. I was smug at first; I knew all about swinging sticks at airborne balls. But about twenty baseballs came flying out of the machine before I made contact with one; by the end, I was sweaty and frustrated. Stop swinging from the wrists, Paul told me; in baseball, we hit from the shoulders. I swung and swung, refusing to believe that my hurling ability would not translate.

Mostly, I forgot about camogie. But somehow, the most satisfying pucks I've ever had were in Boston Common, when my brother Conor visited and I finally unwrapped the hurleys. There was a strange sort of performative glamour to pucking around on the Common. I was never more conscious of being observed as I played – there were lots of confused glances, and a few people were intrigued enough to stop and watch. I felt I was publicly proclaiming my Irishness and my femaleness and my sporting ability.

I visited New York twice during that semester in Boston. The first time was in September, for my twenty-first birthday – I got the Greyhound bus down and slept in a hostel in Chelsea with seven strangers. I still remember coming up the steps of the Port Authority bus station into the humidity of Times Square. There was a huge billboard advertising the first season of *Gossip Girl*, the actors so young and generically beautiful they were almost indistinguishable from each other. They looked down at me imperiously, seeming to promise great things.

The second visit was in December with Paul. He was there on business, and I was mostly free to attend Broadway matinees and hang out in parks and coffee shops while he worked. He brought me to a business lunch at the Spotted Pig, at which I made everyone uncomfortable with my accent and by not knowing what arugula was. Paul's job put him up in a high-rise hotel eerily overlooking what was then still Ground Zero. Later, when I watched the scene in *25th Hour* when Philip Seymour Hoffman and Barry Pepper discuss Ed Norton's fate while looking down into the towers' wreckage, I shuddered in recognition.

I came home, finished my degree, and began plotting a way to get back to the States. Failing at intercounty had given me permission to travel; I had never joined my college friends on interrailing trips or even holidays in the summer months, because I had to be physically present for camogie. Now I felt I could go anyplace, and from there, figure out an identity that was separate from sport.

I took a job at DCU on a one-year contract. A new type of J-1 visa was introduced, whereby new graduates could go to the States for a year to work in their chosen profession. My friend David and I took it as permission to leave. We went to New York and lived in a hostel on Amsterdam Avenue for a month before finding a place on Craigslist: a railroad apartment in Bushwick sharing with an Australian musician named Ellie. It was a good city in which to be Irish, and I maxed out my accent at every opportunity.

I wanted to make it in publishing, but was clueless as to how to actually bring this about. I hopefully printed out copies of my CV and personally called to the offices of *The Paris Review* and tried to hand them to employees carrying coffee cups on their way into the building. I was met with alarm. The internships were already filled, I was told – and anyway, it was all done through the universities.

Eventually I got an editorial assistant job at a literary journal run out of the editor's apartment. Brad loved Yeats and Beckett, and I disappointed him with my skimpy knowledge of both. He had a line drawing of Beckett hanging on the wall. 'I love his face,' I said one day, trying to be somewhat appreciative of my literary heritage. Brad laughed. 'Everybody loves his face.'

My fellow assistants were all graduates of the leafy upstate college where Brad taught. They were all impossibly hip and smart, bringing me to the launches of *n+1* and *Cabinet* and kindly correcting me on my pronunciation of 'Eugenides'. They have all gone on to great things. I still occasionally see their bylines in *The New York Times* and *The Atlantic*; one showed up in an episode of *Girls*.

Brad had three cats, collected rare books and never took the subway. When the workday finished, he would sometimes bring me to the bar on the corner to hang out with his circle of high-powered friends. (I would later get a short story, 'The Recital', out of this bar.) He would fondly make fun of me to the assembled regulars ('I asked her to get a Sharpie from the drawer and she brought me – this is good – a *box cutter*! Isn't that cute?'). But he was fascinating company, and he always bought the drinks.

Early one morning, I watched Tipperary lose the All-Ireland hurling final in an Irish bar on the Lower East Side. It was twenty bucks to get in, and I was the lone Tipperary jersey in a roomful of Kilkenny fans. I drank a beer to numb the pain, emerging blinking on to Second Avenue in the lunchtime rush. It was the first time I felt homesick. When I returned the following Sunday at 9 a.m., hoping to catch the All-Ireland camogie final between Cork and Kilkenny, I found the place shut.

A network of Moneygall expats was always on hand to help out. Tony S. got me a cash-in-hand job at the Irish bar he ran in midtown, and Tony F. – a real estate agent – helped us to find the apartment. One day, Tony F. and I became friends over pucks in Park Slope. He had two hurleys in his apartment but rarely someone to hit the ball back to him. Pucking is a great way to get to know somebody, a strangely intimate mode of communication. You are sizing one another up. You are finding out what they're made of.

'Are you delighted to be home?'

A teammate asked me this, smiling, at my first training session back with Moneygall in the summer of 2010. 'Asked' is probably the wrong word; it was said with the comfortable anticipation of an answer in the affirmative, like 'Are you looking forward to Christmas?' For some in rural Ireland, leaving home is undesirable, something you're forced into for economic reasons. If you do it by choice, it means you have notions.

When my J-1 expired, I hadn't wanted to leave New York. I had been interviewing for publishing jobs for the final few months, trying desperately to garner some sort of security. If I could get a real job, I potentially had a future; if I had an income, I could hire an immigration lawyer. But nothing worked out.

Looking back, New York was a sort of delayed adolescence for me. When I left home for college in Dublin, I'd realized quickly that I didn't have a sense of personal style. Those formative teenage years that most girls spend hanging out with friends and figuring out how they want to present themselves to the world, I'd spent shuttling between school and camogie, between tartan school skirt and O'Neill's tracksuit bottoms, one uniform and then another. I felt a decade behind many of my more sophisticated peers and spent my undergraduate years trying frantically to catch up. Being in New York was the first time I felt confident in who I was socially; the first time when, if someone wanted to befriend me, my initial response wasn't suspicion.

In drafting this personality entirely removed from home, I made mistakes and was probably a frustrating person to be around a lot of the time. But oh, it was liberating. I cut my hair short. I turned down respectable jobs because they didn't seem 'creative' enough. I got into stupid fights with my roommates. I occasionally showed up late to my unpaid internships, once walking in hungover on an editorial meeting to the visible despair of my boss. I walked everywhere. I became proficient at killing the mice that lived in the walls of our apartment. I bought a second-hand bike, which was promptly stolen, then got another one, purely for the thrill of cycling over the Williamsburg Bridge early in the

morning, when no one else was around. I trailed after my
roommate Ellie to her various gigs in Brooklyn bars and
warehouses, drinking PBR and chatting up bassists. I spent
hours in the Met, sheepishly paying a couple of dollars in
lieu of the suggested donation; no one ever batted an eye-
lid. I have a very vivid memory, that terrifies me now, of
climbing up a fire escape to the rooftop of our building
during a house party, with only one hand on the ladder
because I had a glass of wine in the other. I tried to smoke
cigarettes because everyone I knew did, but being asth-
matic I was terrible at it. Many days I ate boxed mac and
cheese for dinner, or a slice from the pizza place on the
ground floor of our apartment building. Most of my earn-
ings came from my job as a coat-check girl in Tony S.'s
midtown bar, and when we closed at 4 a.m. I would walk to
the nearest Bank of America, find an ATM and feed it the
hundreds of singles I'd received in tips. I subscribed to
Netflix, the old DVD-in-the-mail model, and rewatched
the entirety of *The X-Files* on my laptop. I spent hours in
bookshops and wrote several short stories, in a frenzy of
productivity and experimentation that can maybe only happen at the very beginning, when you're figuring things out,
when your potential is infinite. Just before moving to New
York, I'd won a prize for a story I'd written in that first Boston writing class, and now I was interning for a couple of
small but influential publishers; I could sense a future for
myself there, in the world of editors and journals and short
stories and bookstores.

And then, suddenly, I was back in Moneygall, with no job
or independence or instant access to the pulse of humanity
that in New York had only ever been a train or bike ride

away. I missed the subway, descending in one part of the city and emerging in another. I missed the weather. I missed the opportunity to make mistakes. I missed the diversity and the anonymity and the weird, teeming life of it all.

I told my teammate that, yes, I was glad to be home.

6. Club Player

It was, of course, unreasonable for me to be as vexed as I was to be back in Tipperary. My life in New York, while exhilarating, was unsustainable. Coming home was the only option. And I was lucky to have a family home, loving and understanding parents, and sport to come back to.

That first summer home, I slept late, wrote short stories and applied for jobs in the afternoons, and trained in the evenings. In America, I'd had to alter my accent to be understood; now, back home, I was inevitably teased for my twang. I slid back into my soft, slightly nasal midlands voice.

Playing camogie for my club again – with no pressure or aspiration of county – was a tonic. Being a small parish, Moneygall had always struggled for numbers. But there was a strong generation of us. There was Julie at centre-back and her sister Caroline at full behind her; my cousin Mary, by now a lynchpin on the Tipp team; Bríd Byrne, a fearless and versatile player with a great engine, who usually partnered Mary at midfield; Niamh Larkin and Mairéad Teehan, in their teens at the time, and probably two of the most technically gifted players to have ever worn the Moneygall jersey; Sarah Doherty, equally effective as a goalie or a forward; the Kirwan sisters Máire and Michelle, both tough as nails despite slight frames; my sister Eileen at centre-forward, and me on the wing.

As a group, we'd been through the wringer. I'd begun

playing adult camogie at fourteen, when Moneygall was graded junior B. We quickly rose through the ranks to intermediate. From 2002 to 2004 we lost three county finals in a row, the last one a particularly heartbreaking affair, losing to Holycross in Semple Stadium after Eileen had gone off with a broken hand. In 2005 we won the intermediate county title on our fourth attempt. Of the game itself, I remember very little. I scored 2–7 from full-forward, a rare haul. For the goals, one ball was bounced in front of me by Eileen at centre-forward; the other was floated in from midfield by Mary. Gifts.

For me, this win is encapsulated by two photographs which hang in my parents' house. One is the team photo from before the game. There is an age range of about ten years, from Eileen, Bríd, Amanda, Aisling and Sylvia in their mid-twenties, down to Sarah Kirwan, Máire and Michelle's younger sister, who at fifteen was the youngest on the team. Hurling teams rarely smile in pre-match photos, but camogie teams do: even in moments of tension, women are socialized to smile. But no one is smiling in this photo. Every face is focused.

The second photograph is of Eileen and me, red-faced and sweaty after the final whistle, arms around each other, flanked by our parents. I like this photo in part because you can see quite clearly where my sister and I got our features: my face and our father's are strikingly alike, while Eileen resembles our mother. All four of us are beaming with joy and relief.

Shortly after I got home, we played a newly promoted team we'd never played before. Camogie was not their club's primary pursuit. 'Typical football team,' said our mentor at half-time, and we all nodded sagely. We had been thumped, bruised and physically intimidated in the first half. The ref threatened to send off my opposite number if she kept doing what was doing; she kept doing what she was doing.

'Hey,' I said to her after one incident, where she punched me squarely in the chest as I moved past her with the ball. 'Don't fucking hit me again.'

The f-bomb dropped awkwardly between us; I was trying to be tough, and she, a Tough Girl, could sense that this didn't come naturally to me.

'You fuck off, would you,' she said, with such withering disdain that I was rendered momentarily speechless.

'Yeah, well. If that's the only way you can beat me, then fine,' I said primly.

She rattled off another string of expletives that made me feel once again like a lowly first-year student who'd happened upon the cool girls smoking in the toilets. But she didn't hit me again.

I kept looking for work. My dad drove me to Dublin, Galway, Cork and Limerick to drop off CVs at local businesses. I finally found a job in a bookshop chain in south county Dublin. I moved into a house share near one of the less glamorous DART stops and took the train to work each day, taking solace in the cliffside scenery. I read ferociously on the commute, and on my lunchbreaks. In the evenings I wrote, often fuelled by coffee or wine, or got the DART into town to see college friends or attend a book launch – hopelessly glamorous events to me, where you might spot quite famous writers having a drink and a chat. The accessibility of writers in Dublin was always shocking to me, as was their grace and patience when accosted by an admirer.

I continued to travel home every weekend from March to September for training and matches, in a '99 Renault Clio gifted to me by my mam when I returned from the States. The steering-wheel vibrated and rattled under my hands when I pushed it on the motorway, but it did the job. But as I became more involved in Dublin's writing community, taking up a postgrad in creative writing, I began to resent those weekends at home, the time expended, the tanks of petrol. And yet I felt I owed it to my clubmates, my family, my squandered potential, to keep coming home. The dream of the senior county title persisted. Every year we would perform decently in the championship with our bare-bones squad, getting to the quarter- or semi-final before being eliminated by Drom or Toomevara or Cashel. I made a few half-hearted attempts to train with teams in Dublin midweek, but never found any consistent routine. My fitness and performance deteriorated. I was there in body but not in spirit.

This has always been the quandary for rural graduates: do you move to Dublin, where the jobs are, or try and find something closer to home, family and hurling? If the former, how long can you continue the hurling commute home; how long before you transfer to a city club and raise your kids as Dubs? If you choose the latter, are you cutting yourself off from work and social opportunities purely for a devotion to an amateur game? And if you're the person trying to hold a rural club together – how do you manage it when most of your teammates from eighteen upwards are scattered to the winds?

In what was maybe a manifestation of my ambivalence towards the game, I stopped using ash hurleys when I returned from the States. I seized on my sister's Cúltec hurley, which she had bought just to try it out. Founded in 2008 in Ferbane, Co. Offaly, Cúltec makes its hurleys from a composite of epoxy, nylon and graphite. The Cúltec packs a ferocious belt that belies its lightness, and for a forward in particular its powerful puck – loaded with backspin – lent me an advantage I felt I couldn't refuse.

They're also convenient for being unbreakable, and for always being the same length, weight and shape. Living in Dublin, using the Cúltec exclusively allowed me to bypass the cottage industry of hurley-making and hurley-fixing; one less element of GAA tradition to maintain. Before, I would have bought four hurleys at the start of the season and grown attached to one or two, only to have them break in a match – or worse, training – thus necessitating a visit to the hurley-fixer, and starting the whole process again. With the Cúltec, I bought one at the start of the year and it would see me through the season. Often they lasted even longer, with some light wear and tear on the grip and the bas, but I still treated myself to a new one at the start of each year, like buying new stationery for going back to school. I only ever truly broke a Cúltec once: it snapped in the middle during a clash ball, but still didn't separate into two pieces, instead forming a hinge that I could open and close.

Composite hurleys are disdained by many, on the grounds that they have none of the spring or variety of the bespoke ash hurleys that a traditional hurley-maker will provide. The sound out of the Cúltec is the shallow slap of plastic rather than the more resonant clash of ash. The sameness of Cúltec hurleys is both a blessing and a curse: a blessing because a new stick takes no time at all to get used to, a curse because you miss out on the ritual of trying a new hurley out – examining its grain, gently flexing it against the ground to test its spring, holding it at arm's length to feel its weight, searching for that impalpable feeling of 'rightness'. I've never noticed any issues with accuracy that I've heard others describe, but the touch of a Cúltec does take some getting used to; it's somehow bouncier than an ash hurley, and the ball is liable to shoot out of your sphere of influence when you put the stick to it.

Native Irish ash stock has been devastated by the ash dieback epidemic that started in 2012, and ash is increasingly imported, but ash hurleys are still by far the most common stick you will see on the pitch. The Cúltec is used by a handful of elite players, such as Tipp's Orla O'Dwyer and Dublin's Ryan O'Dwyer, and it has always surprised me that it hasn't caught on more widely. This is probably partly to do with the Cúltec's infamous precursor, the Wavin – a plastic hurley launched in 1977 which by all accounts gave the hands a ferocious sting anytime you went in for a clash. But it is almost certainly more to do with superstition and tradition.

I met Cal in 2013. We did the long-distance thing for a while, but the following year, as I was in the midst of being priced out of my Ranelagh boxroom, we decided to move in together in Cork city, where there was a vibrant writing community and rents were much cheaper. We moved into a flat over a busy intersection in the city centre, an almost-trendy street where restaurants always seemed to be on the verge of opening up or closing down. I'd left Dublin behind but bypassed home; the drive back to Moneygall was actually a little longer, now.

Just to see, I emailed a couple of clubs in the area to find out when they trained, and asked if they would mind me joining a couple of their sessions to keep up my fitness. I had no particular affinity to any of them; Moneygall had played against Douglas a couple of times in the Munster league, but beyond that my knowledge of Cork clubs was sketchy. Colette from St Finbarr's got back to me the next day, telling me their timeslots for training and saying I'd be welcome to join in. In March 2015 I went to my first session. Nervous in the dressing-room, I did what I always did: drew out the process of getting my socks and boots on, then pretended to be absorbed in my phone. But my eyes were drawn to the framed team photos hung high on every wall in the dressing-room. The colour combination always leapt out at me, no matter where I saw it. The Barrs wore blue and gold.

I was twenty-eight in 2015, the year that I began training with the Barrs. That spring, I lined out at centre-forward for Moneygall in the first league fixture of the year, at home against Silvermines. There was a low mist, making it hard to see anything below knee-level, and conditions were slippy. I was marking Joanne Nolan, who I've known for years from various county setups, and we were having a torrid time of it. Just before half-time, she turned to me and said: 'Eimear, I'm getting too old for this.'

Joanne is a year younger than I am, and I knew what she meant. I was beginning to make notes for an essay about camogie, and typed into my phone's Notes app in the dressing-room: *This is the first year in which I can reasonably expect to be marking players ten years my junior.* Once you start noticing the age gap, it's impossible to unsee. There's the dressing-room banter that makes you feel like a dinosaur: talk of mocks, debs, CAO forms. And you notice it on the field. You are heavier than you were ten years ago: living away from home and enjoying yourself, you've got fond of takeaways, buckets of cinema popcorn, tenner bottles of red wine. In a twenty-yard dash, the willowy teenager with the high metabolism will beat you. So you compensate. Learn to throw a hip or an elbow in front of your marker the split second before the ball breaks. Learn to sidestep and shimmy to eke out the yard or two of space you need to strike.

It's all circular, it's all karma. As a young slip of a thing, I used to love skipping past older wans who struggled to change direction. Now it is my turn to be that older wan.

As a kid, one of the players I most admired was Claire Grogan, who was born the same year as me. She won an All-Ireland camogie title in 2000, at the age of fourteen. This is no longer allowed – you now have to be sixteen to play senior camogie, even at club level. But it is still fairly normal for a senior club team to have at least a handful of

teenagers, and certainly several college-age women. Players in their mid-to-late twenties are considered veterans;
players in their thirties, who might be settling down and
thinking about kids, are retirement risks. This tendency
towards youth is part of why I was so hard on myself at
seventeen and eighteen, when I couldn't handle the pressures and demands of intercounty camogie. I didn't make
allowances for my age because all around me there were
girls the same age, and younger, handling it just fine.

I thought I would become less self-critical with age. I
haven't, though the nature of the auto-critique changes.
You are hard on yourself not out of insecurity, but because
you have watched and played the game long enough to
know what actually makes a good performance good.
Your standards for yourself are higher than ever, but your
body is less and less capable of delivering. The mistakes
haunt me more. Everything good I do in a match can only
be recalled in a blur, but blunders I make now have a startling clarity in remembrance. A time I should have called a
teammate back to cover an opposing player, who ended up
getting a crucial score. A time I shot for a point and missed,
when I could have carried it forward more, chanced a goal.
It's only when you can see the end of your playing career
approaching that you start to brood, start to worry your
old mistakes like scratching a favourite itch.

I used not to be haunted by errors. I used to shrug them
off, or at least hold them in balance with all the good things
I did. Next ball, next match, next season. As a sportsperson, you need this sense of constant forward momentum
and optimism. During my teenage summers, I had training
or a match practically every night of the week. You have

too many teams to play for, too many demands on your time, so you're less likely to dwell on things, but the potential for burnout is huge. A couple of my teammates and I were playing for the adult club team when we were fourteen – which meant we were also playing under-14, what used to be minor (under-16), and under-18. Four teams, and that was only with the club.

When you're older, however, you usually have only one team – maybe two, if you're playing intercounty – on which to peg summer hopes. It focuses the mind. Now that I only have a few years of playing left, winning has never meant more.

Then there's the physical wear. Being an older player means taking an anti-inflammatory after a match, especially if you've taken a knock. It means a post-match visit to the pool or the sea – as a necessity rather than an indulgence. It means bruising more easily and slathering yourself with Arnica after training to minimize the black and blue patterns on your arms. It means going down when hit, as much to take a quick rest as to try to win a free.

You can never have all the attributes at once. You can't combine the boldness of youth – the risk-taking, the fitness, the lightness on your feet – with the craftiness and experience of age. But nearing the end of your playing career injects a bit of urgency into you. You can see the end in sight, and you want to make these last few years count. You have better vision and awareness of the players around you, a stark contrast to the tunnel vision of youth. You have more perspective, a stronger temperament. You're inspired by the confidence and enthusiasm of the players you train with, even if some of them are literally half your age. Training goes from being a chore to something you actively look forward to and take glee in. Where else does a grown adult get to canter around a field after a ball?

7. David and Goliath

For my first holy communion, my godfather Declan, my mam's brother, gave me a lavishly illustrated children's bible. Though the cover depicted a pastel Jesus dividing up loaves and fishes among a benign crowd, the contents of the book were heavily skewed towards the Old Testament. It was a treasure chest of pestilence, martyrdoms and tyranny. I devoured it.

One of my favourite stories was that of David and Goliath. During a standoff in a valley, the fiercest Philistine warrior, Goliath, challenges the Israelites to send out a champion, to settle the conflict by single combat. Saul, the Israelite king, is expected to face Goliath, but he is afraid. A teenage David – a musician in the camp, not even a soldier – volunteers, taking with him only a sling and five river stones. The rest you know, or can guess.

Most artistic representations of the story depict David holding Goliath's severed head. The full-page illustration in the children's bible, however, was different. In the background, but still dominating the image, was Goliath – monstrous, haughty, loaded with armour. In the foreground with his back to us, David: wiry, shirtless, sling slack in his right hand, gearing himself up to strike. I loved the slingshot: as a six-year-old, it felt accessible to me, and reminded me of another great underdog myth, that of Setanta and the hound. David and his sling, Setanta and his hurley: these stories indicated that at the end of childhood, there would be a reckoning, a monster to slay. (I would also have a fraught, tragic boyfriend, in the vein of David's bestie Jonathan or Cúchulainn's rival Ferdia.) I'd be challenged to single combat, or locked out of a feast, and would have to do what was necessary with the tools to hand. It didn't seem scary to me: the weak would always overcome the strong, I was sure of that.

Growing up in Moneygall had inured me to the status of scrappy underdog. In the early 2000s, the Moneygall hurling team fought its way to two senior North Tipp finals, facing Toom each time. I remember those finals vividly, painfully: the buzz of the buildup, thinking 'why *not* us?'; the dogged, hard-fought rucks in summer heat; the savage joy when Moneygall slotted away goals; the second halves, when the Toom cogs would start turning; the widening gulf in the scoreline; that old familiar victory lap. There is a popular fallacy that teams who have not traditionally known much success are 'hungrier' when they arrive at a big occasion, and therefore have some kind of advantage derived from their desperate need. The reality is that there is a knack to winning. If you have won before, it's easier to do it again, those neural pathways and muscle memories providing a template for yet another victory.

When you're always chasing the game and nobly losing, that becomes your default state. When you're always defending a lead, you become ruthlessly proficient at it. The small team that wants to pull off a shock win has to invent a method to win on the spot, but the team that's used to winning simply has to repeat entrenched habits and patterns.

Half an hour to the south of Moneygall is Thurles, home to Sarsfields, the most successful club in Tipp's history with thirty-six senior county hurling titles to their name. The dominance of Thurles makes a certain sense: as one of Tipp's biggest towns, with a population in the thousands rather than hundreds, they have a much bigger pool of players to draw upon than their rural neighbours. There are, however, constraints placed on a club's reach.

Before Moneygall camogie club was set up in 1995, local players went elsewhere – Toomevara, maybe, or over the Offaly border to Shinrone. These clubs, like many of the other leading camogie clubs in the country, drew players from multiple neighbouring parishes. Moneygall – like other new camogie clubs that were established in partnership with single-parish GAA clubs – was at a disadvantage compared to the long-established teams, with their large player pools. Often, the newly-formed teams naturally tried to convince players to transfer to their new home club, putting those players in a difficult position: choosing between the club where they had a history and a set of relationships, and the club based in their home parish. A player wishing to make such a transfer could not be prevented from doing so; but not every player chose to do so.

League of Nations, one of my selectors used to call them: those long-established Tipperary camogie clubs like Drom and Cashel that pulled in players from far and wide. Moneygall, by contrast, organically hewed to the parish rule by pulling from the same schools, villages and families as the hurling club. We were proud of our parish status, of our clannishness, of the quality players we produced despite our size.

We were a team of schoolmates, neighbours, sisters and cousins. We were a tightly bonded squad: most of us had grown up together and had been playing hurling with one another, on both a casual and an organized basis, for years. We knew we were at a distinct disadvantage numbers-wise, but we wanted to prove a point. What we lacked in a player pool, we told ourselves, we would make up for in excellence and culture.

Of course, for this to be a true David and Goliath story, David would have to win in the end.

In 2006, our first year up in the senior championship, we encountered two strong neighbouring teams, linked, as we were, to hurling clubs: Burgess and Portroe. These teams featured players I knew and admired from my time playing at various levels with Tipperary. Burgess had Sinead Nealon, Therese Brophy, and the McDonnell twins Eimear and Deirdre. Portroe had the O'Halloran sisters, Jenny and Trish. Both teams had bigger pools to draw from than we did, and when we met them, they generally beat us; but they also gave us something to aim for. In five, ten years, we said, we could be like a Burgess or a Portroe: a strong, competitive, community-based senior team.

Then, in 2009, we heard that Burgess and Portroe were merging. They were struggling for numbers, they said. We were aghast. How could they be struggling for numbers, we asked ourselves, when we – a smaller community – were able to field a team?

They named themselves Duharra, an old name in Burgess parish. They won the senior county title in 2010, only their second year in existence.

I can guess at why they did it. Two neighbouring clubs with that number of county players between them, that amount of All-Ireland medals? They must have looked at Cashel, Toom and Drom and wondered why they deserved all the spoils. Players nearing the end of their careers looking at their medal display, and the county was all that was missing.

I understand this impulse. My All-Ireland intercounty medal means little to me because I did little to earn it. The county club championship was the one that mattered.

We had our run-ins with Duharra down the years. I had great time and respect for many of their players, especially Therese Brophy, who had taught with my parents and took me under her wing when I joined the Tipp panel. Dee McDonnell, too, had shown me incredible kindness by giving me lifts from Dublin to Thurles for training. And Eimear Mc was a hero to me. I'll never forget her directive to players out the field before crunch Tipperary games: 'Get the ball into me, high or low, I don't care.' I wanted to be like her, with that level of confidence in my ball-winning abilities, my potential to do damage.

But they didn't respect us. One year, when we went to play them in Burgess, they used both sets of goals to warm up. The convention in camogie and hurling, as in most sports, is that each team takes half of the pitch to prepare before the game. But that evening, the Duharra forwards shot for points at their own end, while their keeper came down to the Moneygall end with a few others to be put through her paces, just yards from where we were warming up. The message was that this was their turf, and we would get no hospitality there. The disrespect stung.

In 2015, we beat Duharra for the first time in a league fixture in Moneygall. We had new management that year – Tom and Diarmuid, two local guys who had hurled with distinction for the Moneygall senior team – and there was new energy in the squad. We had occasionally beaten Burgess or Portroe down the years, but never the entity known as Duharra. They were county champions three years running and we'd finally cracked them; we knew, now, they weren't infallible.

Walking off the pitch afterwards, buzzing, I overheard one Duharra player say to another: 'This is like winning a county final to them.'

Looking back over my camogie career, I don't have great recall. I blame this partly on having played so many matches at so many levels, especially as a teenager. Some of the years blur together. I also know that my dad remembers every match in granular detail, so I've outsourced my memories to him, and can ask him to remind me at a moment's notice. There are a handful of games, however, that I remember in stop-motion detail. The 2015 county semi-final against Duharra in the Ragg is one of them.

I remember the tension in the crowd, on the sideline, among the players. The constant jabbing from my player off the ball. My dad always taught me that if your marker hits you, it's a sign of insecurity and weakness; they know they can't outplay you and so have to resort to fouling. This usually allowed me to shrug or laugh off any belts I might receive. But in this game it was so constant, so prevalent, that I did something that even now makes me cringe: I hit back, several times.

I remember peeling off Niamh Larkin on to the left

wing in the first half and receiving the pass to pop over an easy point. Settling, feeling good. I had a year's worth of Barrs training behind me at that stage and was playing better than I had in years.

I remember looking at their sideline and seeing at least a dozen subs togged, compared to our six or seven.

I remember Tom running in to me at wing-forward to give me an instruction. My cousin Mary, in front of me at midfield, was contesting the puckouts; she won some cleanly but others were being swept up by Duharra. Drop to midfield for the puckouts, Tom told me; let Mary break it and then you gather the loose ball and deliver it in. I did as he said, and it worked like a dream.

I remember, in the second half, blocking a girl down and then winning possession and getting a free and the blood roaring in my ears.

I remember shooting for a point off my right, rushing it, the ball shaving the outside of the right post.

I remember when they copped on to my puckout tag-team with Mary and started to choke midfield with bodies. I stopped winning easy ball. For one of our puckouts, a Duharra girl floated between myself and Mary. I should have called to Mary to drop. The words were in my throat but never made it out. The Duharra girl collected the puckout and put it straight back over the bar.

I remember Niamh Larkin being unstoppable that day, roofing it midway through the second half, just as Duharra were starting to pull away from us.

I remember being with them, with them, with them the whole way. They couldn't shake us off and they were rattled.

I remember that Julie was marking Eimear Mc, a long-time friend and teammate. Towards the end of the game, they nearly came to blows.

I remember we were down a point in the dying minutes. My cousin Gráinne, Mary's younger sister, won the ball on the endline, and handpassed it to me on the edge of the square. I was on the ground before I could finish it. Penalty.

I remember Mairéad Teehan stepping up to take it and Diarmuid running in with instructions. She took the point. Mairéad is one of the most talented players to ever wear the Moneygall jersey: she could have buried it. (But what if it had been saved?)

I remember the heat that day. At the full-time whistle we gathered in a huddle, took on as much water as possible, readied ourselves for extra time. 'We have them, lads,' I said, and meant it. We went again.

I remember feeding the ball in to Niamh on the edge of the square; she scored under ferocious pressure. Mairéad's frees were unerring. We were still with them at the break.

I remember they got a couple of soft frees in the second half of extra time. Tapped them over. I resented the ref for granting those placed balls to them, the team that were supposed to win. It happens all the time.

I remember them jumping and hugging one another at the final whistle, while we all held back tears. Our best performance ever, 80 minutes of hurling, and it wasn't enough. I had always been stoic in defeat – you learn to be, as part of a small club – but not this time. This time, I had really believed.

*

They went on to win the final, lacing our wounds with salt. In some ways it made it easier, knowing we'd come within two points of the county champions. In some ways it made it much harder. We could have stopped them. We could have been champions.

At the time of writing, Duharra has nine county titles to its name, including a record-breaking streak from 2012 to 2018. Interestingly, Portroe have since seceded, playing the 2022 season as an independent club at junior B level. Meanwhile, the 2022 junior A county champions are none other than Moneygall. Having lost senior status some years ago, the club is now resurgent once again.

Looking back, you can't blame the players or even the club itself. You can only blame the Camogie Association's all too malleable rules, which allow club boundaries to wax and wane at will – not just to survive as a club, but to dominate.

Forget nine county medals. I just wanted one. But if there's one thing sport teaches you, it's that you're not entitled to anything.

An rud is annamh is iontach. A uniquely Irish phrase, not just in language but in attitude. We're a post-colonial nation, and in many ways we don't expect – or even, in a stubborn way, *want* – too many nice things. Going without will make the having, whenever it comes along, all the sweeter. That's the reasoning, anyway. It's why culturally we love when teams end famines and are deeply suspicious of anything more than a three-in-a-row.

Is there any joy in dominance? I'm sure that players with multiple medals would say yes, plenty. I have never followed a team at either club or county level that won every year. Not to be a Goldilocks of All-Irelands, but the Tipp hurlers' three wins over the course of the last decade felt *just right* to me. I'd only be starting to wonder if we were losing our relevance when another title would come along to quell my anxiety.

The weekend before Christmas in 2020, I watched the Dublin men's footballers beat Mayo in the All-Ireland football final for the fourth time in eight seasons. The following day, the Dublin ladies' footballers beat Cork by five points in their final. A six-in-a-row followed by a four-in-a-row. Watching the two games play out, it was striking to note the similarity of approach in both Dublin teams: a methodology, a calmness, an athleticism, almost an inevitability to the way they play. 'Of course,' you found yourself murmuring as Carla Rowe slotted away her penalty, or as Con O'Callaghan boxed in a goal. 'Of course.' This is what they do.

So often, the narratives that we use around sport serve to reinforce the status quo. When we say that a team 'showed why they're champions', what we're really saying is that they deserved to win because they have won before. When we praise a strong, successful team for their experience or character, we're implying that their opponents – often an emergent team – did not display these qualities. It's rarely that simple.

I asked my dad what it was like to live through the early sixties, when Tipp won four All-Irelands in five years. 'Well now, that was a bit different,' he said, citing Tipp's Munster final loss to Waterford in 1963, which interrupted the streak and proved them fallible. I guess that is how you find joy in dominance – by thinking of the times when the team wavered or failed, only to come back stronger than ever. The low points are how we orient ourselves in victory; how we see the triumphs in sharper relief.

8. The Transfer

While 2015 wasn't the breakthrough year we hoped for, it still represented Moneygall's best year of camogie to date. Afterwards, things fell apart, in the most benign way possible. Three of our top players had wonderful personal news: they all became pregnant with their first child. In their absence, the backbone of the team was hollowed out. In 2016, we didn't win a single championship game, going from our best season to our worst in the space of a year.

I experienced those matches as if I were moving through treacle: balls falling short, passes intercepted, moves that simply didn't come off. I felt as if I was floating above the games, unable to impose myself on them. We tried to play as we had the year before: moving the ball quickly down the wings, into space, in front of danger-women Niamh and Mairéad, relying on our fitness and aggression to win the individual battles. When it's done well, moving the ball in hurling is as satisfying as a trapeze act: the timing of movement, swing and catch is everything. But we kept missing our connections. We were overstretched, and didn't have anyone experienced enough to fill the gaps. Mary dropped to centre-back, where she excelled, but that created a void at midfield.

Since I'd started training with the Barrs in the spring of 2015, I had observed them without key players periodically through injury, travel, or work commitments. It wasn't unusual for players to go on holiday during the summer and miss a game or two, whereas in Moneygall, going abroad during championship was considered a cardinal sin. (I remember Bríd returning early from a holiday in Italy in 2011 to play a league final; we lost.) When the Barrs were missing a player, there was enough depth in the squad that there were two or three girls competing to fill the gap.

As I settled into the training routine at the Barrs, there was some good-natured teasing from the management and players. 'I have the transfer papers ready to go,' Mick Ryan, the coach in my first year, would say. As soon as Moneygall were knocked out in 2016, the Barrs manager, Ellen Clifford, wondered aloud why I couldn't transfer to play in the Barrs' championship game the following week. It was jokey but serious at the same time: the suggestion was there, a standing offer.

We exist in a tribal system in the GAA. Club and county allegiance isn't chosen, but designated at birth. As in any team sport, the emphasis is on the collective rather than the individual, but the GAA's ethos of amateurism and volunteerism intensifies this outlook. It simplifies motivations: we take part in the sport first and foremost for the love of it, and as long as the team succeeds, nothing else matters. In media discourse, players are likelier to be depicted as 'servants' to their country than as stars.

The cornerstone of this way of life is the club. As the tagline of the AIB All-Ireland club championship goes, it's 'one life, one club'. GAA players believe fiercely in the idea that growing up in this parish rather than that parish shapes our identity in some essential way. There is a sense of continuity that comes from playing in the same colours as your father and your grandfather. When family members come to watch you play, you feel the weight of that tradition, the sense that you are a link in an unbroken chain. Your club colours are your club colours and they will always look right to you, the way a loved one's name will always sound right to you, regardless of who bears it.

All of these things are true, all of them weighed heavily with me. But I was demoralized from our poor season in 2016, feeling that we would never again get near a county final. The commute from Cork city to Moneygall – a round trip of three and a half hours – was starting to wear on me. And I now had a viable alternative. Substituting your club of origin for another one closer to where you live may seem soulless, the prioritization of convenience over meaning. But I was making friends at the Barrs, beginning to think of them as teammates. I was becoming invested in their fortunes, carrying hurleys and water on the sideline for their championship fixtures.

That winter in Cork, I began to seriously consider a transfer. It took me a while to even acknowledge to myself how I was thinking, longer still before I said it out loud. Cal was the first person I suggested it to, and to him it made sense. He had never watched hurling before we met, but developed an appreciation for it through exposure, as I learned to appreciate soccer from watching games with him. As our relationship grew, we began to parse the many norms, assumptions and values that our respective upbringings gave us – upbringings that were inevitably influenced by the sports we played, watched and loved. He has always been slightly bewildered by the GAA's claims to place, boundaries and belonging: how we will allow the happenstance of the parish in which we were born, something we had no choice or control over, to dictate our lives. How we will accept the need to leave for work or study, but can't countenance playing our sport elsewhere. The GAA's amateurism has always struck him as exploitative rather than devotional. And to me, soccer's professional model seemed cynical and opportunistic. Even the word 'transfer' sounded wrong to my GAA ears. But the more I talked it out, the easier the decision became. It came slowly, piece by piece. But I had to keep justifying it to my own GAA-addled brain, kept having imaginary conversations with my family and teammates back home. Transfers were rare in Moneygall and were occasionally controversial – the result of a falling-out between a player and management, say. No matter how reasonable I told myself *my* transfer was, I was still entering into that contentious space. The point that I landed on, that I felt no one could contradict, was that I was making a selfish decision: prioritizing myself before the club. In any conversation I had, I would need to own this stark fact. I would always be from Moneygall, but I would never again be a Moneygall person in quite the same way.

There are two statues of Christy Ring in Co. Cork. One is at Cork Airport, where Cal used to work and where I'd often pick him up after a long shift. This is the better of the two, in my opinion: Ring is angular, kinetic, poised to strike, his face creased in concentration. It's slightly marred by a plaque on a podium that is positioned too close to the statue and ruins the aspect, but as a representation of a hurler mid-play, it's great. I have a photo of myself standing next to it from August 2014, when Cal and I were searching for an apartment to rent. I'm standing in the shadow of Christy's steel hurley, my cardboard coffee cup balanced on the base of the monument, giving two uncertain-looking thumbs up.

The other statue, at the GAA grounds in the town of Cloyne in east Cork, is bigger and more flattering. Christy stands atop a seven-foot pillar with the inscription *Chriostóir Ó Rinn, 1920–1979* – though a Google search reveals that when it was originally unveiled in 1983 by former Taoiseach Jack Lynch, Ring's teammate, it simply bore the legend *Christy Ring*. With a popped collar, pronounced chest muscles and his hurley held by his side, Christy looks more relaxed here than the coiled hurler at Cork Airport, as if he's walking in the parade before the match instead of playing in it. I have photos with this statue too, taken on the way back from trips to Ballycotton or Garryvoe. This Ring looms over you.

Christy Ring – the most iconic player in GAA history – is also a player who transferred. Even more controversially, he transferred intra-county: from Cloyne, where he was born and grew up, to Glen Rovers in Blackpool, Cork city. In the RTÉ documentary *Christy Ring: Man and Ball*, aired in December 2020, Bunty Cahill, a neighbour and friend of Ring's, says: 'There was some falling out anyway.' Donal Óg Cusack, a Cloyne man, allows one to read between the lines: 'I never felt it rested easy on the people who were talking about it . . . It wasn't a conversation that I very often heard anything about.'

Denis Coughlan, who hurled with Cork and the Glen, says diplomatically: 'There would have to have been a great understanding from the people of Cloyne.' A narrative that everyone seems to be able to agree upon is the economic factor: there was more work in Cork city than in Cloyne, and the 30km drive was not a manageable commute in those days. Ring transferred in 1941, at the age of twenty-one, and won a county medal in his first year, playing alongside Jack Lynch, Jim Young and other luminaries.

Cusack has unusually commanding screen presence and, with footage of Ring relatively scarce, he provides the documentary with many of its most memorable moments. Early on, he walks down Spital Street in Cloyne, home to both the local church and the GAA pitch. Christ on one side of the road, Christy on the other. 'It was like there were two gods,' Cusack says. 'I'd be praying to one god that he might make me more like the other.'

At the close of the documentary, with a crack in his voice, Cusack describes the modern-day Cloyne crest. Like most GAA crests, it features a football and a pair of crossed hurleys. The date of formation, 1887. The club colours of red and black. Two crosses to represent the town's two churches, and a local landmark, the round tower. At the apex of the crest, a star. As Cusack explains: 'It's got a star that represents Ring but within the star there is a little tear and what that tear represents is the fact that Ring had to leave Cloyne.' Your club of origin will always claim you, but they'll never forget that you left them, either.

18/01/2017, 10:14, Eimear wrote:
Hi girls,
  Just a quick note to let ye know that I've decided to transfer to the local Cork club for 2017.
  It was a really tough decision to make. My main reasons are that I'm probably going to be based in Cork for the foreseeable

future, and I've found the travel tough enough the last few years.
Also, last year was a difficult one in terms of morale/lack of
matches. I know this year is already shaping up to be more
positive, but I still want to try something different.

    Sorry to be messaging ye like this – I really wanted to tell ye
in person over Christmas, but I wasn't around Moneygall too
much in the end. With plans now being made for the 2017 season,
I figured I should let ye know sooner rather than later.

    Hope ye can understand, and looking forward to catching up
with ye soon.

    Eimear xxx

18/01/2017, 12:35, Julie wrote:
Hey eim! Thanks for your msg! I was getting worried about you
alright when you were quiet on camogie group chat! Obviously
we're going to miss you SO *feckin much eim!! But I can totally*
understand your reasons! I've no doubt it was a very difficult
decision for you as you're a very proud moneygall woman !! Xx

                                     Eimear:
        Thanks Jules, you're v kind! I'll miss ye loads too x

Bríd:
Hi Eimear. Caroline and I were only talking bout you yesterday.
I'd be lying if I didn't say I was disappointed but at same time can
totally understand your decision. You'll be missed x

                                       Eimear:
      Thanks so much for understanding, Bríd. I get your
        disappointment, I've very mixed emotions about the
            whole thing myself. I'll miss the team so much x

18/01/2017, 14:22, Mary wrote:
Hey Eim! Oh man times are changing . . . I'd pretty much repeat
what the girls have said . . . was wondering what your position
would be alright but can completely understand your decision,
and know you wouldn't have made it lightly . . . thanks for the
message . . . you certainly will be missed x

Eimear:
Thanks a million Mary! Will be supporting &
rooting for ye big time. Girls, thanks so much for
your understanding & soundness. Ye're the best. Xx

I left with as little fuss as I could, on the hinge of the season, in the hopes that some people might not notice my absence. I was nervous of how my teammates would respond; I had anticipated a rift, for people to no longer want to talk to me, a fear that was more reflective of my own paranoia than the temperaments of my teammates. In the end, I was humbled by their kindness and understanding. But the guilt remained. I had a very keen sense that while I was making the right decision for myself, I was betraying Moneygall: depriving a small rural club of another player, giving up on the dream of making it to a county final. To abandon ship before that goal was achieved felt like a betrayal of a common cause.

My father made it a bit easier. He has devoted most of his life to Moneygall hurling: first as a player; then as a local teacher creating a hurling culture in the primary school; then as an administrator and volunteer; then as a coach, trainer and selector at multiple levels, in both hurling and camogie. In GAA terms, he taught me everything I know.

He raised us in Moneygall, steeped in its values. But he has – perhaps more so now in retirement – a tendency towards expansiveness, towards accommodation, towards saying: 'Well, why not?'

Since transferring, I've become highly conscious of the little differences between urban and rural clubs. Urban clubs are more likely to have a clubhouse, a place to gather and drink after matches; rural clubs go to the local pub. Rural clubs usually have a stand; urban clubs are more likely to use any spare land for an additional pitch. Urban clubs have the simple advantage of being situated in a more populous place, of having a larger pool to draw on. There is also, counter-intuitively, more togetherness in an urban club: players are likelier to actually live nearby, and it's much easier to gather the core of the squad for a mid-week session.

Of the 2016 census, the Central Statistics Office noted: 'The decline in persons aged 19 to 25 years in rural areas, as young adults move away to study and work, is a strong feature of the rural population . . . Women in their 20s are more likely to have moved into urban areas than men, while there are more men than women living in rural areas.' For every 1,000 women in their twenties living in rural Ireland, there are 1,054 twentysomething men, suggesting that urbanization affects rural camogie teams even more than it does rural hurling teams.

With the Barrs, at the age of thirty, I began playing better camogie than anything I produced in my twenties. It was thrilling and it also made me sad that I didn't get more out of myself during my physical prime. I was now training twice as much as I did with Moneygall; competition for

places was fierce. After years of coasting, I started thinking of myself as a finisher again. My confidence soared.

Our first league game in the spring of 2017 was at home.
I sat stewing in pre-match nerves in the dressing-room
where I'd only ever prepared for training before, my red
Moneygall gearbag standing out in a sea of blue Barrs gear.
I was thrown the number 15 shirt and pulled on a Barrs jersey for the first time. Before giving her team talk, Ellen
presented me with a pair of blue and gold socks, like the
ones I wore with Tipp all those years ago. She welcomed
me to the club and the dressing-room broke out in applause.
I ducked my head, mortified, delighted. This, too, could be
a home.

9. The Barrs

In February of 2018, I began working in an entry-level admin role at UCC. I worked in a departmental office with three other women, and my main responsibilities were to accept assignments from students, perform filing and photocopying for lecturers, and keep the stationery cupboard well stocked. The department had its own kitchen/canteen overlooking the university's quad, where I sometimes ate lunch and made several cups of lemon and ginger tea each day. To get to the kitchen from our office, you had to walk down a corridor, then through a social area, then down another corridor: three sides of a square. The walk probably took less than a minute, but it strangely became something I looked forward to every day: a break from the static nature of desk work, a chance to get out from under the gaze of students and colleagues and the clock.

Every day, on that short walk, I imagined myself on the camogie pitch. I tried hard to walk normally, but there was probably a certain bounce in my gait, a flexing of my fingers. I visualized stretching to catch the ball, landing, pivoting. I pictured soloing and using my left hand to fend off defenders. I pictured smashing the ball to the roof of the net, over and over again. I did this at least five times a day, five days a week. I've probably never played better than I did in 2018.

The previous year – my first year playing for the Barrs – had been a cultural transition. The Moneygall dressing-room had always been relatively quiet; players chatted, but we were all midlands girls, soft-spoken and modest. The Barrs dressing-room was cacophonous. Cork people have a reputation for flamboyance, but I had to see it to believe it. In the midlands we were all about shyness, deflection, hiding behind our long straight Manson-girl hair; my Cork teammates had swagger, directness and obvious self-esteem. While I couldn't quite relate to it, I aspired to it.

The Barrs grounds, too, began to feel like home. In no way did it resemble the pitch in Moneygall, which was surrounded by green fields full of mature trees and grazing cattle. The Barrs was on the industrial outskirts of Togher, adjacent to the South Link, a busy six-lane road. Planes appeared low and big in the sky over the pitch, drifting into the nearby airport. And for whatever reason, the moon was almost always visible over the grounds, even when it was still bright outside.

You drive down a cul-de-sac lined with housing estates. You turn right into the car park, which is always overflowing, and muscle your way into a space. You walk past the clubhouse bar, where wins are celebrated and losses drowned. You go into one of the low-ceilinged dressing-rooms that run along the sideline of pitch 1 – the best of the three – and get togged. Hopefully you're training on pitch 1; if not, your coach will direct you to pitch 2 down the back, which has floodlights but also swarms of midges which bite in the summer; or pitch 3, which is uneven and usually assigned to the kids' teams. Along the way you'll pass the four astroturf courts, again populated with kids' teams or middle-aged lads playing five-a-side. The place buzzes with life.

Our new manager was Brian O'Sullivan, a former Barrs hurler who was involved in the Cork intermediate camogie setup. From the start of the 2018 season I was dropped in at full-forward, a position I grew to love. I relished the responsibility of it: being the target woman, being almost obliged to score. We entered into the most intense training regime I'd known since my Tipperary days: three times a week, starting in late January, on the astro and in the gym at first, then graduating to the pitch.

In the spring, Brian took me aside after training one day. He had two questions: was I interested in joining the Cork intermediate camogie panel? And second, would I consider becoming captain of the Barrs?

I was taken aback, on both counts. That Brian believed in me was very gratifying; because of the experiences I'd had down the years, I knew that a manager's backing was a rare and valuable thing. I told him I would get back to him on the Cork intermediate front, though I knew I would decline: I was happy at the Barrs, assimilated, and the thought of being the new girl all over again exhausted me. I'd played in two intermediate All-Ireland finals for Tipperary, in 2003 and 2004; we'd lost both. (The Antrim and Galway jerseys I received in exchange for my Tipp shirts on both occasions are still regulars in my rotation of training gear.) The transfer to the Barrs had caused me sufficient internal consternation; I wasn't sure if I was ready to transfer counties, too. 'My dad would never forgive me,' is what I told Brian: a white lie.

I had been captain of the Moneygall senior team just once, when I was twenty-six; I had assumed I just wasn't captain material. I told Brian as much, but he disagreed.

'Your attitude, your commitment, the way you carry yourself in training?' he said. 'You're a natural leader.'

I was resistant. 'Do you have a shortlist?'

'Yes, a shortlist of one!'

I went away to think about it. A blow-in in her second season being handed the captaincy: I knew that some of the girls wouldn't like it. The duties of the captain are few and ritualized: pick a handful of grass and throw it in the air before a game to determine the direction of the wind (in Ireland, there is always a wind); go in for the coin-toss with the opposing captain before the match; and accept silverware on behalf of the team should the occasion arise. It's more symbolic than anything else, but still it means something.

My friend and teammate Pam Finn encouraged me, however. 'No one is perfect,' she said, reasonably. 'Why *not* you?'

The biggest reason I could think of was that I'm an introvert, and dislike speaking up in a group. Numerous teammates have told me that they can't hear me on the pitch, even when I feel like I'm screaming. A therapist once observed that my words seem to catch in my throat; when I'm anxious, I feel as if my chest is closing up. Though Brian assured me that being captain did not mean speechifying in the dressing-room, I knew it was expected. 'Eimear, I know you're quiet,' my teammate Lynda said at a break in training in the spring, 'but we need to get better communicating as a group, and that has to start with you.'

It's not that I'm a bad communicator; it's just that I'm better in writing, where I can order exactly what it is I want to say. But sport is built for verbal communicators. I've always preferred to communicate through my actions or through one-on-one chats. Speaking to the room – even when it's full of friends and teammates – fills me with dread.

Equally, I hate telling people what to do. It stems from past experience – of having teammates yell at me or, occasionally, yell en masse at the team in the guise of a tough-love pep talk. It's interesting to see how people handle power; often, they use it to lash out. And the tough-love method, designed to motivate the recipient, can just as easily backfire and demoralize. 'Some players need anger to perform, and some need praise,' Keeva McCarthy, one of our best forwards, said to me once. We agreed that we both perform better with encouragement as our motivator rather than tough love. Still, I always found it easier to take criticism from management than from my fellow players – perhaps because it's understood that it's their job to do that, and feels less like a betrayal, a violation of trust. If I feel like my teammate has lost faith in me, then I lose faith in myself; it poisons the well.

The story of 2018 is not the story of me finding my voice, learning to speak up or becoming an inspirational leader of women. That's something I still struggle with, something I'm still working on. For me, 2018 is the story of my left knee.

We barrelled through the league between March and June. We were determined and aggressive, and it was exhilarating to be part of that campaign. When we went behind or things didn't go our way, we were generally able to find a solution and claw our way back into the game. Brian and his backroom team had instilled a sense of belief and confidence that meant that we didn't panic on the ball or drop the heads when we made mistakes. We found ourselves in the league final, the first final of any kind for several years, with the prospect of the team's first title since winning the county championship in 2006 – an occasion that was commemorated by Lynda and Rachel Myers, another of the team's stalwarts, with 'Barrs 06' tattoos (Lynda's is on her calf, Rachel's on her shoulder).

In the final we met the Glen, the Barrs' traditional rivals from the north side of the city. They'd beaten us in the league's preliminary stages and the teams knew each other well. I was pulled down in the square early in the match and took the resulting penalty, a poor effort that was saved. There was a tit-for-tat aspect to the game; we finished level, went to extra time. In the first half of extra time, I caught the ball in the square and turned for goal. The hurley was pulled out of my hand; I kept running until I could handpass it past the keeper. (You could do that in those days: the handpass goal was finally outlawed in 2021.) I took too many steps, for sure, but the ref overlooked it, maybe because I'd been fouled. I was glad that the goal stood, not to have to take another penalty. We were three up at half-time of extra time, but the Glen pulled back three points to level it up again.

The replay was a comedy of errors for me, personally. Having gotten us off to a good start by scoring an early goal, I proceeded to hit wide after wide (including, unforgivably, from scoreable frees). But we did enough, and won by two points, and in the post-match photos I'm beaming so much that my face is crumpled up. The Barrs hadn't won silverware since the mid-2000s, and neither had I. Winning felt good, and I felt we were primed for more of the same.

Two weeks after the league final victory we played our first championship round against Muskerry, a divisional team – that is, a grouping of junior and intermediate clubs who join forces to field a team in the senior championship. (Amalgamations: the bane of my existence.) We were brimming with confidence. I scored an early goal and felt vindicated, somehow: this felt like confirmation that we were going to continue crushing any opposition we encountered. We only led by a point at half-time, but the sense of invincibility remained. It's a paradox: confidence is essential when playing sports, though too much of it can slide you down into the murk of complacency.

We lost that game by a couple of goals, and were then drawn to play Douglas in the losers' round. We played well that night, I thought: not flashy but steady, building up a five-point lead in the second half. A freak goal from Cork star Katrina Mackey out on the left wing brought them back within two about ten minutes from the end; then Julia White, another Cork star and one renowned for crucial last-minute scores, equalized in injury time. Another replay.

Sunday morning training, a few days after our draw with Douglas. We take to the pitch at half nine. I'm always a bit groggy at this hour, the first coffee of the day not yet metabolized. As part of our warmup, we play a game of tag: half of us tuck yellow bibs into the waistband of our shorts, and the other half give chase, grabbing for the bibs.

I am not yet warm. Normally I would stretch before training, but I overslept. I shift my weight on to my left foot and feint, trying to evade someone, and then I hear it: a *clunk*. It is neat, almost satisfying. I feel it, too: something in my knee being displaced. I crumple to the grass. Gráinne Cahalane is facing me when it happens, and I can see from her expression that it doesn't look good. I limp to the side-line and sit down, my two legs stretched out in front of me. The left knee has swelled up and stiffened already, and is fixed at an awkward angle: I can't make the back of my knee touch the grass.

Kevin, our S&C coach, tries to cajole me, telling me the swelling will more than likely go down overnight and I'll be back at training on Wednesday. I don't think this is true, but don't have the capacity to argue.

I'm bounced from appointment to appointment: doctor, clinic, physio. Strings are pulled to get me seen sooner – such is the clout of GAA clubs – which makes me feel grateful and guilty. The doctor puts me in a brace that limits the knee's movement. The clinic takes an MRI scan, which confirms that the medial ligament has a grade 2 tear. I am referred to a consultant.

I go to the physio expecting to be given a rehab programme. I am holding out hope of coming back, if not for the Douglas replay, then for the championship match after that. I know what Cork and Barrs powerhouse Gemma O'Connor did after suffering the same injury in the previous year's All-Ireland semi-final. She worked incredibly hard to be back for the final two weeks later, and not only did she get through the game, she defended brilliantly, scored an inspirational point in the closing minutes, and collected her eighth All-Ireland medal. If Gemma could do it, maybe I could too.

But the physio does not give me a rehab programme. The ligament is one thing, he says, but there is a tear in the cartilage too. If I played, and worsened that tear, it could be career-ending. 'You're an adult,' he tells me. 'It's up to you at the end of the day. But the potential dangers outweigh the benefits, in my opinion.'

I try to train with the knee brace on. I feel awkward, lumbering. I can sense the other girls' hesitation when I'm on the ball: no one wants to tackle me. Eventually, Kevin tells me to just rest it, that I'm doing more harm than good.

So I step out of training. I stand on the sidelines and I hate it: you're cold, you're bored, you're wildly envious of everyone running around, expressing themselves physically. Attending training while injured is regarded as good form, a way of ensuring that you're still involved, but it can be dispiriting. My time standing on sidelines – and there has been a lot of it, in recent years – has convinced me that I would not be a good manager; first, because there is a lot of standing around in the cold, and second, because you have to impose standards such as 'injured players must attend training'. How do you set standards across the board, while also reckoning with the fact that every player is temperamentally different and what works for one won't work for another?

I receive conflicting advice. One physio advocates for the knee brace; another says that it causes the muscles in the knee to lose strength, to rely on the extra support, and delays recovery. When I'm referred to a doctor and explain that I have a match coming up, one of the first things he says is, 'Look, I'm not going to give you a shot the day of the match.'

The night before the replay against Douglas I get strapped: my knee is wrapped tightly in a network of bandage and tape, in such a way that allows movement but also gives support. I am doing this on the off-chance that we're in need of a goal and I can be put on the edge of the square in the last five minutes, but deep down I know I'll be a liability out there. It certainly wouldn't make sense to put me on ahead of any of our subs, all excellent hurlers and fully fit.

We lose the replay on the night of my birthday. I pace the sideline, feeling utterly helpless. The only contribution available to me is by way of a pre-match motivational talk in the dressing-room, and even this I fumble. I think: *This is how it must feel to be a manager or coach; you're utterly invested, you are playing every ball in your mind, but there is very little you can do in real terms.*

There are better days ahead: the following season, in 2019, we will win our first championship match since 2016. We'll get all the way to the semi-final, losing to eventual champions Sarsfields. I'll play every match that year: some games I'm able to make my presence felt, some not so much. But it's infinitely better to be on the pitch than off.

Two months later, when I still can't fully straighten my left leg, I go in for surgery on my meniscus. The winter is spent in the gym, rehabbing it. It's my first experience of serious injury, but it won't be the last.

10. Sidestep

The first practice match of the 2020 season is at home, under lights, against our neighbours and rivals the Glen. It's early enough in the year that my hands are still liable to rip, palms opening up against the friction of the hurley. They became soft over the winter without my realizing – too many long bubble baths, too many applications of handcream.

In the match, I'm astonished at how slowly I am moving. Winning the ball in a ruck, I will myself to step out, shrug off my marker, but it's as if I am swimming over the grass instead of running.

I have never actually been fast, but I've always had a good sidestep. Or as my dad once told me: you don't have the legs, but you have the feet. Thirty-three now, one of the oldest on the panel, and even the feet are deserting me. You can blame the soft ground but that only goes so far. I console myself by thinking of the weeks of training ahead, the long and short sprints, the ladder drills, the mobility work. I think: I'll be up to speed in no time.

2.

Then: the pandemic. No matches, no training, no gym. I don't even have a wall. Growing up in Tipp I had my pick: the gable end of the house (classic), the front wall of the shed, and the converted garage, a nice windowless stretch. But the walls of my rented terrace house in Cork are pebbledash, the rebound untrustworthy.

On my daily 2km-radius walk, I quickly realize that all the viable walls in the locality belong to other people's houses. I can't imagine they would take kindly to the *thunk . . . thunk . . . thunk.*

In the end, I order one of those rebounder nets for the tiny back yard. The yard has been an ongoing project since we moved in, over three years ago – full of scraggly shrubs and moss-covered kerbs and low, cunning walls. It's hard to swing a hurley there, much less a cat. Cal assembles the rebounder, like a mini trampoline propped on its side. I try a few pucks and am hooked by the fuchsia bush. I tell myself it'll be fine, I just need to adapt, to shorten my grip.

Every morning I go out after breakfast and don't allow myself back inside until I've struck and caught ten balls in a row off my left and ten in a row off my right. The coffee is often cold by the time I come back in.

3.

A couple of years ago, I sort of got into running. I bought decent running shoes and ran a couple of 5 and 10k races, before a knee injury gave me an excuse to avoid pounding the hard pavement.

Now I dig out the old Asics. The radius rule lends itself to running, to testing your boundaries. I start by jogging to a nearby park, planning to do five laps and run home again. This, I calculate on Google Maps, will amount to 5k.

I give up after three laps.

Laps don't work, I've found, if I'm trying to make myself run a certain distance. I have to eliminate any opportunity to cut corners. I have to take myself far enough away from home that I have no choice but to run all the way back.

I decide to run to the club. Check in on it. It turns out it's exactly 2.5k away from my house. Run there, run back. Simple.

On a summer's evening, the club would normally be packed. The overspill from the car park would be lining the road. All three pitches would be on the go, and probably all four astros. Kids at the ball wall, oul lads at the bar. Now, the gate is locked.

Later, I'm scrolling through Twitter when I come across Elaine Buckley's stunning opening sequence for the new season of *The Sunday Game*. Shots of abandoned pitches and rugged coastline are intercut with iconic GAA scenes. I'm generally not very sentimental, but when the words *this too shall pass* appear on screen, my eyes begin to smart.

4.

For the first summer in as long as I can remember, my body is bruise-free. Without three training sessions punctuating my week, I begin to feel unanchored, the days of the week even harder to track. On the WhatsApp group, Brian texts us weekly training programmes – pushups, sit-ups, lunges, squats. I do them in my bedroom in the long narrow space between wardrobe and bed, missing my teammates, the feeling of shared pain, the collective expenditure of energy.

We're all trying to retain a base level of fitness, in the hope we'll get a chance to be glad of it later in the year. We're watching what we eat and drink, trying to keep the touch in. We have to be ready to go back to training at a moment's notice. We try not to think about the alternative possibility – that all our efforts will be for nothing.

∫.

In an attempt to boost my morale, I watch a coaching webinar delivered by former Tipp hurling manager Eamon O'Shea. A professor of economics, O'Shea is unself-consciously intellectual and given to philosophical tangents; he drops the word 'metaphysical' in the first five minutes. His love of the game is obvious, as is his insistence that love of the game must be central to any approach to hurling. 'When you're coaching a young fella, or a young girl . . .' begin many of his sentences, and I smile at the inclusion: these little things matter.

I scribble down notes as I watch, thinking I might type them up later, make something of them. Reviewing them, I realize that the snatched phrases have a jazz-poetry qual-ity to them. I start rearranging the lines, experimenting.

Quarantine must really be getting to me: I think I'm a poet now. Or that Eamon O'Shea is.

6.

I've been keeping a diary of everything I've watched, read and listened to since Friday 13 March, when everything shut down. Tana French crime novels. TV shows like *Buffy* and *30 Rock* that I've seen many times before. Hilary Mantel's *Wolf Hall* trilogy on audiobook which, with its depictions of the lethal sixteenth-century 'sweating sickness', hits a little too close to home. Several podcasts about murder. Far too many cooking shows.

Cheer, Netflix's six-part documentary series about a college cheerleading team, hits me in a way that I wasn't expecting. There are several reasons to enjoy *Cheer*: the larger-than-life personalities, the Texas accents, the incredible routines that are closer to Cirque du Soleil than anything involving pompoms. But it's the devotion of the cheerleaders themselves that really gets to me. These kids – they're all in their late teens or early twenties – train for several hours a day, week in week out, to compete in a sport so niche that most people aren't even aware that it *is* a sport. They train harder than any club player, certainly more than me now, sprawled on the couch watching Netflix between Teams calls. They strive to reach the national college finals. For cheerleaders, varsity competitions are the end of the line. There is no professional league to join. After a couple of years of intense dedication, of sprained ankles and concussions, they graduate and that's it. In

Gaelic games we sometimes talk about sacrifice and commitment as if we have a monopoly on these virtues, but maybe we haven't even scratched the surface.

7.

It's pretty rare for Gaelic games to be depicted in a film or TV show. Perhaps the most infamous example is the opening scene of the 2011 thriller *Blitz*, in which Jason Statham beats up three carjackers with an old, crusty-looking hurley, but not before describing the sport itself as 'a cross between hockey and murder'.

Normal People's Connell Waldron, now arguably the world's best-known Gaelic footballer, was originally a soccer player in Sally Rooney's novel. Director Lenny Abrahamson, perhaps after learning about actor Paul Mescal's background as captain of the Kildare minor football team back in 2014, made the clever decision to make Connell a Gaelic footballer instead, and in the process exposed the sport to a global audience.

Rooney's novel includes an insightful passage about sport and the emotional expression and release it permits, particularly among young men:

> Back in fifth year when Connell had scored a goal for the school football team, Rob had leapt on to the pitch to embrace him. He screamed Connell's name, and began to kiss his head with wild exuberant kisses. It was only one-all, and there were still twenty minutes left on the clock. But that was their world then. Their feelings were suppressed

so carefully in everyday life, forced into smaller and smaller spaces, until seemingly minor events took on insane and frightening significance. It was permissible to touch each other and cry during football matches. Connell still remembers the too-hard grip of his arms.

By contrast, Connell hides his love of reading from his friends, aware that revealing arty inclinations or even thoughtfulness will break some sort of social code. Internally, he checks himself for becoming too engrossed in books: 'It feels intellectually unserious to concern himself with fictional people marrying one another. But there it is: literature moves him.'

'Just finished Normal People,' tweeted Joseph O'Brien, AKA @Joe__90, in May 2020, when we are all collectively binge-watching. 'Great show but completely unrealistic that Connell wasn't once hounded by Carricklea to go back and play for the club.'

8.

Webinar
After Eamon O'Shea

Some things are important
beyond outcome.
Get out of the way.
Reconcile omnipresence
& invisibility.
The incredible

lightness
of being.
The ball has to be central.
Teach the grammar
of the game.
How does it make me one
with myself?
(I love the ball.)
You'd be surprised at how
basic training is at intercounty level.
You have to allow for
ego & creativity,
& remember –
we can give praise
for free

9.

Art – by which I mean books, music, movies, TV and video games – has always been as much a lifeline for me as sport has, and yet I've never really been able to combine the two. I don't really talk to my sporty friends about art, and I don't really talk to my arty friends about sport. I'd been writing for about eight years before I dared to write about camogie.

To quote a popular meme, *one does not simply* write about the GAA. When you lift that lid, you end up writing about your childhood, your family, your community, your iden- tity, and how you feel about all those things. Your whole life is on the table.

But there was something else, too, that gave me pause: a fundamentally different way of *being* in each of the two worlds. Good writing comes from a place of vulnerability, but that's not where good camogie comes from. In art, you can be yourself, warts and all. Exploring the light and dark in yourself, and by extension the human condition, is essential. But in sport, you have to be a better version of yourself, an idealized version. Faster than you look. Braver than you feel. Stronger than you know, deep down, you really are. It's only by behaving in this way that you can achieve excellence – by acting as if you're already there.

10.

Throughout the day, my laptop is with me constantly, like a loyal pet.

In the mornings and afternoons, I put in a shift. I work at the kitchen table; Cal works upstairs in the spare bed-room. I can hear his muffled Teams calls through the ceiling, and I'm pretty sure he can hear mine, floating up the stairs.

When the day job is done, I try to grab an hour or two to work on my own writing. If I'm cooking dinner, the lap-top will be there on the kitchen counter, streaming a sitcom or a favourite movie, something that provides diversion without requiring my full attention. The evening might bring a Zoom call with friends or a session of Yoga With Adrienne on YouTube to wind down. I even do my sets of pushups and situps in front of Netflix, because god forbid I be left alone with my own thoughts for half an hour.

Throughout all of this, Twitter will be open in a tab, and it's hard not to dip in and out of the stream of bad news.

My laptop has become my portal to the world, but my eyes are tired and my back complains. It's at moments like this I miss training the most, for its physical unshackling. I can be in a tense or anxious mood but at training, my shoulders relax. My jaw unclenches.

Camogie gives me an opportunity to be physical, to be *big* in a way that is not otherwise available. Quarantine, on the other hand, asks us to be small, contained; to keep out of the way. When I go for walks at the Lough or in the park, I'm perplexed by those who insist on walking three abreast down the narrow pathway, who make no effort to maintain distance from others, who would nearly jostle you as they pass.

But the sidestep is coming in handy. The sidestep is back.

11. On Injury

You want to hurt yourself in the warmup. Not too much, of course. Just ease into the physical discomfort, start building your resilience. Catch enough raspers so that your left palm tingles and you're not flinching when the first high ball lands in the match. Get a couple of shoulders from your teammates so that you're not rattled when your marker does the same. Get the blood flowing.

During the summer, bruises map the narratives of each match and session. Backs get hit on the legs, while forwards get hit on the arms. Backs block the ball with their bodies, or get hit by nippy corner-forwards swinging desperately at stray balls, hoping to poke them goalward. Forwards get swung at while soloing towards goal. You feel the belts but they don't get sore until later, when the adrenaline turns off like a stuttery tap. Sometimes I feel the need to cover the bruises up. People look, sometimes, particularly in cities; the man at your side gets stern, suspicious glares. My teammates schedule their weddings for the off-season, so their skin will be unblemished in photographs.

Bruise audit, 2 August 2019:

- Right foot: Two small round bruises on instep from studs. Brown.

- Left leg: Four large bruises down the outside of my calf. Slaps from various clashes, goalmouth melees. Purplish-yellow.
- Right forearm: Large fading bruise. Slap of a hurley while running through on goal. Yellow.
- Right shoulder: Arch-shaped bruise. Slap of a hurley under a high ball. Blue-purple, i.e. recent.
- Left shoulder: Archipelago of bruises down to elbow. Not sure what happened here but probably multiple belts under a high ball. Blue-purple.
- Breastbone: Small fading bruise the size of a two-euro coin. No low-cut tops for a while. Yellow.
- Left forearm, underside: A small arch-shaped scar from a cut incurred during training in February. Fading slowly.

My favourite sliver of Cork slang – a lexicon that puts many other counties, including Tipp, to shame – is 'haunted'. It means fortunate or lucky, which struck me as counter-intuitive at first, but now feels apt: not all ghosts are malevolent. *We got inside just before the heavens opened*, you might say, *we were haunted*. Or: *I was haunted, I got the very last parking spot in the whole place.*

(Another nice piece of Cork slang, and equally open to misinterpretation, is using the verb 'to read' to mean criticize. It originates, I'm guessing, from the practice of being 'read from the altar', or named and shamed at Mass, if one didn't donate enough to the collection or otherwise stepped out of line. 'I was reading your sister,' I said once to my teammate Lynda, whose sister Barbara O'Connell is a sports reporter. Her response: 'What do you mean you were reading her?!')

For the first two decades of my playing career, when it came to injury, I was haunted. I never had anything worse than a pulled muscle, never had to sit out training for longer than a couple of weeks. This was unusual; nearly everyone I played with had broken at least a finger at some point. On the pitch, I'd witnessed broken wrists and hands, dislocated shoulders, torn cruciates and Achilles tendons. A broken jaw, once. But aside from the usual litany of belts and bruises, nothing ever came for me.

Once I hit my thirties, however, it was a different story.

2020

In that first pandemic summer, we were allowed to return to training in June. In July, a week before the first championship match of the season, I sustained a partial tear to the anterior fibres of the ACL on my right knee. We were in the midst of a tough Friday night training session: hot sun, hard ground, plenty of sprints. My knee felt sore when I decelerated out of the sprints and turned to jog back to the endline, but it was only when I was walking off the pitch afterwards that I started to worry. My leg felt *heavy* – dead weight, like I was dragging it around the place.

It hadn't popped like my left knee had two years previously, so I thought maybe it wasn't as serious as all that. But still, it shook me. This was the good knee, not the dodgy one.

When I woke the next morning, I knew I had done

something terrible to it. I was stuck to the bed, and the leg felt remote, like it no longer belonged to me. If the good knee could be compromised, what was next to go? An ankle? A hip? An entire limb?

I got injured at what would normally be the height of summer hurling season, but this being 2020, we'd only been back training five weeks. I'm sure my story was a common one, up and down the country. Club players, having missed out on those first crucial months of training, tried to make up for lost time and went too hard too soon.

I began the work of trying to salvage my season. I went to my GP, to physios, to a consultant, and for an MRI scan, always with the same questions: When can I go back? When will I be right?

There's a fundamental disconnect between injured players and the medical professionals who look after them. The consultant or the physio is thinking about what the knee will be like when the player is sixty – will it be functional? Will it be a source of chronic pain? Will it need to be replaced? Meanwhile, the player wants to know if they can play championship next weekend.

There was conflicting advice. The physio advised against strapping the injury or using a knee support, telling me it only helped mentally, not physically. My GP looked bemused when I repeated this opinion back to her. 'Try it, and see if it helps,' she said. And it did help – mentally or physically or both, I can't be sure.

Luckily, I didn't need surgery; the tear to my ACL would scar up and heal by itself with time. My physio gave me a programme and I got to work. Anyone who has done a programme of rehab exercises knows that they are tedious, but that's what Netflix is for. Over the course of the summer, I squatted and lunged my way through all three seasons of *Hannibal*. In retrospect, I could have picked a less gruesome show to watch while trying to build up my knee, but maybe I needed something visceral. Something involving body horror.

The world has to be negotiated differently when you're injured. It's a bit like making a cup of tea in someone else's kitchen: you have to stop and think about each step instead of doing it automatically. But there are lessons in injury. You learn the parts of yourself that require more work and support. You try to find other ways to contribute to your squad, besides playing. You learn patience.

I came on in the last fifteen minutes of our county quarter-final and scored a goal. It was more of an icing-on-the-cake goal than a vital one, but it felt incredible. I had thought I was gone, finished, but this proved there was still a kick in me. It being lockdown, our games were filmed for livestream, and I watched the goal back, rapt, more times than I care to admit.

There was an odd sort of glamour to the year, with club players able to watch their own performances, many for the first time. At first it was a little bit *unheimlich*, like seeing your own face on screen during Zoom meetings. You'd think: do I really run like that? Is my swing/pick/handpass really that awkward? Is that what my teammates have been looking at for years? But then you warm up to the sight of yourself. You get used to your own awkward gait, the idiosyncratic swing. You get to see yourself in a whole new light: in the same way you've been watching your heroes on *The Sunday Game* for years. All at once, there were

YouTube channels and Facebook livestreams for every game in every county at every level in every code. I was able to watch not only my own squad's matches, but also my siblings' games back in Tipp. The sometimes home-spun quality of the commentary added to the charm: it was hard not to be won over by commentators who could maintain the utmost professionalism for the majority of the game, but then roar 'G'wan Johnny!' when their team won a ball on the edge of the square.

I was brought on again during our county semi-final against Inniscarra. I got one golden chance, a ball down the wing from Ella Wigginton-Barrett, one of our most promising young players. I took it, rounded my marker, and struck for a point while a back closed in on me. It was so scorable. The ball shaved the right-hand post, and the Scarra crowd on the bank behind me cheered. I never watched it back, but over the course of the winter, when I closed my eyes, that was the moment I replayed and relived.

2021

'No injuries in 2021!' This was my mantra when we came back training as a group in April, the line I'd spout to any-one who would listen. We had been training on our own since January: running twice weekly, recording our routes on an app for accountability; doing a weekly Zoom work-out with Natasha Varian, a personal trainer and the best high fielder on the squad.

It was a relief to be back on the pitch, to be together again, but two of my three previous seasons had been

marred by injuries picked up in training, and I was determined to be available to play for the entire year. I had no
expectations that I would be starting games – I was thirty-
four, and had missed most of the previous year – but I felt
that I could play a role. I wanted my workrate and ball-
handling to be at their peak. I wanted to be a reliable scorer
or free-getter, to be a good option to be sprung from the
bench. These were my modest hopes.

The previous three years, I'd noticed that it took me
ages to get going. Even in 2019, my golden injury-free
year, I spent much of the league panicking that I had lost
it, whatever 'it' was. I felt off the pace, I wasn't scoring, I
got frustrated with myself. My mentors reminded me of
the things I was doing well – winning the ball, distributing –
and told me the rest would come. In June, just in time for
championship, I hit my peak, but it had taken five months
of hard training to start performing well. I didn't have the
luxury of that lead-in time after the pandemic hit.

So I struggled early in 2021. I played okay in a couple of
league fixtures and practice matches, winning frees and
giving assists, but I failed to register a single score. Then,
in July, I had one of those golden training sessions that get
you bursting out of your skin. I caught ball, I picked out
teammates perfectly, I scored a few tasty points. Finally, I
thought, I'm back in business.

I had, meanwhile, picked up a lockdown hobby. My
partner and stepson are both skaters, and I got bored of
sitting on a bench watching them whizz around skate
parks, so I invested in a Penny Board – a small plastic
cruiser rendered in primary colours. During the first lockdown, when time seemed to flatten and stretch out in a

way that it hadn't since childhood, I went out to the Marina several days a week to skate the flat, tarmacked walkway that stretched along the river. At first I was mortified, thinking I'd fall flat on my face, that people would tut and roll their eyes at the sight of a thirtysomething on a child's toy. But there were so many other awkward adults out there, on rollerblades and rollerskates and scooters: everyone reclaiming a piece of childhood, trying something new. I loved it. I found joy and freedom in doing something publicly that has no obvious function besides fun, and that I was not any good at.

It was mid-July, and we had a league game against Inniscarra in the evening. I finished up work early. I was itching to play and it was a beautiful afternoon. Cal was working remotely and still had a couple of calls, so I asked Seb, my thirteen-year-old stepson, if he'd like to go and play basketball.

There are three public courts in the city that we play at: Douglas, Togher and Ballyphehane. We visited them all in turn, but they were all either commandeered by soccer players or vandalized and unplayable. There were skateboards in the boot of the car. Come on, I said. Let's have a roll around.

The skate park in Ballyphehane is small but serviceable. There were a bunch of kids, Seb, and myself. Parents stood at the edge and chatted, but not me: I was a Cool Stepmom. I participated. I avoided the ramps, though; I just skated endless circles. It was my comfort zone. But then I saw a couple of pre-teens roll down a ramp and thought, *What the hell. If the kids can do it . . .*

I had no idea what I was doing, but I went into it

believing nothing bad could happen, that my wholesome
new hobby would never backfire on me.

I went down the ramp and the board slipped from under
me and shot away. My right foot came down, hard, on the
ramp. I looked down and saw my foot splayed to one side,
the bone coming through the skin on the inside of my
right ankle.

I won't be able to play the match was the first thought that
registered. Then, children crying and running. Three of the
parents rushed to my side, one of whom (fortuitously) was
a nurse. Seb found a blanket out of nowhere and draped it
over me. A pool of blood gathered under my ankle. The
parents kept talking to me, worried that I would pass out. I
went into shock: the pain was dull, but my breath was fast
and panicky. Later, I would be amazed at the lengths to
which the brain and the body will go to protect the self.
The ambulance came quickly, and I was given a little vaper
of laughing gas. I was told that I had a high pain threshold;
had I ever given birth? No, I said, I just play sport.

I was hysterical by then, and laughing. I texted Marian,
one of our selectors, to say I couldn't make the game. At
Cork University Hospital, they popped my dislocated
ankle back into place. I would need to be operated on:
between my ankle and shin bone I had three breaks, and
there was a chance I would need a skin graft for where the
bone came through my skin.

I was on a trolley in a corridor, then moved to a ward. I
couldn't bring myself to the bathroom so, after some initial resistance, I used a bedpan. With the aid of drugs, I
slept. The next morning, I was told I'd be brought to surgery, so I was nil by mouth. At 4 p.m. they told me that the

surgery had been postponed to the following day; I glugged down several bottles of water. I had books and podcasts and movies on my phone but no real desire to engage with any of them. Because I was in the one position all day – on my back – sleep was hard to come by.

The next morning I was wheeled to theatre. The arrow they drew on my thigh wouldn't wear off for weeks. When I woke up, my right foot was in a heavy, knee-high boot. I didn't need a skin graft in the end, which was a relief.

I was brought to a ward. The heatwave had hit, so all the curtains between beds were kept open, all day long. There was no privacy. I was haunted to be next to a window. There were four other women in the ward, all of them elderly and there long-term. I felt like an interloper. The nurses came around and asked us all loudly – some of us were deaf – if we'd had a bowel movement lately. There was an elderly patient opposite me, whose call button had been disabled because she used it so often. Now she addressed me, in distress: *Ring the bell! Oh please, ring the bell!* I did it the first couple of times until the nurses told me to stop.

The nurses were kind, but it was also the case that to them, I was a problem to be solved, a machine to be monitored, a quantity of dead weight to be manoeuvred around safely. *I'll lug the guts into the neighbour room*, I thought, every time a nurse helped me to the bathroom. Looking back, I was amazed at how readily I submitted to the condition of being a patient. Pride evaporated on the ward.

I read a true-crime book called *Unspeakable Acts*. I watched season 4 of *Angel,* the *Buffy* spin-off, comfort viewing from my youth, and streamed championship matches on my phone. I listened to Big Thief, *My Favorite Murder,*

Trashy Divorces, Tomberlin. Because of Covid regulations, I couldn't have visitors. On the third day, there was a minor disaster when one of the nurses unplugged my charger, scolding me that it was a fire hazard. From my position in the bed, I was able to grab the charger's wire when needed, but the socket itself was out of reach, and I didn't yet have the wherewithal to get out of bed and plug the charger into the wall. My phone – my TV, my music player, my connection to the outside – died quickly, and it was several hours before I could convince a different nurse to plug the charger back in for me.

The physiotherapist came around to show me how to use crutches. Not only could I now bring myself to the bathroom, I could have a shower, sitting down, with a plastic bag duct-taped to my thigh. I eagerly filled in my menu choices for the next day on a slip of paper, a small opportunity for agency, though all the options were equally terrible.

I was kept for a week, because of my open fracture; they wanted to make sure that it didn't get infected, so I was on a drip of antibiotics most of the time. One sleepless night, they couldn't get a needle into me. A young doctor tried, her hands shaking. She was only fresh out of university. After two attempts, she apologized; I could tell she was trying not to cry. Eventually, an American nurse named Carrie found a vein.

I have a picture from the day I came home from hospital, taken by my mother. I'm splayed out on the couch at home, my leg in a cast; Cal sits next to me on the arm of the couch. It is the happiest I've ever looked.

12. Hurl Like a Woman

1. *Femininity*

I have never felt very good at being a woman, or rather, at performing femininity. As a child, I hated wearing dresses: it meant I couldn't ride a bike or perform cartwheels. The buckle-up shoes my mother wanted me to wear to Mass hindered me from running and climbing.

Later, in my teens, I found that my fine, flat hair resisted the step-by-step hairdos in the pages of *J-17*, and the homemade face masks of lemon juice and mashed banana did nothing for my acne. Earrings and necklaces were fine, but rings and bracelets impeded my hands. I resented the 2000s midlands beauty standards that dictated I wear heels and fake tan to go to the nightclub in Nenagh. I couldn't walk in heels, my feet battered and tender from hurling boots, from constantly running on hard ground. I hated the smell of fake tan, the faffing around with the mitt in the bathroom, my inability to apply it without streaking.

In my twenties, I disliked the fact that in order to appear professional, I was expected to wear a full face of makeup and perfectly blow-dried hair. These morning routines cost me time and money, and because I wasn't especially good at them, I only ever achieved presentability, never beauty.

I could not believe this was my inheritance, my job as a

young woman. Even now I get nervous before weddings, at everything you're supposed to remember: outfits, shoes, hair, makeup, nails. So many ways to fall short.

At every stage of life, I've been surrounded by girls and women who passed with flying colours where I faltered; who had not only mastered the trappings of femininity, but enjoyed them, saw them as avenues of self-expression. I never thought these women – many of whom were and are my friends – were shallow, but I did find them intimidating. How could they find joy and empowerment in something that made me feel like such a failure?

(What if what the bullies said about me was true? What if I *was* like a man?)

Going to America was a huge relief. In a multicultural city, it felt ridiculous to try to change the colour of your skin. In Brooklyn, where I lived and socialized, femininity was what you made of it. And in a city with a strong queer culture, gender norms were not as stringently enforced. The girls I met had tattoos and brightly dyed hair; they wore short dresses that flared at the waist but paired them with Converse or Vans. I felt utterly at ease in this hipster aesthetic, with its gestures towards the skater and grunge scene. Gendered clothing felt like an option, something to play with, rather than a baseline requirement. I cut off most of my hair and no one cared. After I returned home I kept it short for a while, but had to field so many questions about it that I soon grew it out again.

All the while, I nursed a suspicion that my sportiness was at the heart of my ambivalence towards femininity; that, if nothing else, female athletes simply did not have the *time* to worry about their appearance too much, did not have the patience for the rituals of womanhood. But that was a smug projection on my part. If I actually looked around the dressing-room, I would see the manicures, the pedicures, the threaded brows, the French plaits, the fake tan.

I find it fascinating that some women seem to groom specifically *for* sport. Makeup sweats off. Tan can be marred by mud, blood and grass stains. I have a visceral memory of helping a teammate to cut off her manicure in the dressing-room with a pair of kitchen scissors: elaborate nails are generally a hindrance when you're trying to handle the ball. Why bother? Is it that many women present so femme in everyday life that it inevitably bleeds into sport, as a matter of habit? Or is there a sense in which we're grooming ourselves primarily for other women – for the female gaze more than the male?

Women who play team sports both subvert and transcend gender norms. To play sport as a woman is to telegraph – sometimes indirectly, sometimes unknowingly – that you are not satisfied with the gender roles that have been laid out for you: to be gentle, passive, caring, accommodating and supportive of the men in your life. Playing against other women simply for the savage joy of physical competition has nothing to do with men, and that is one reason why there are men out there who are deeply suspicious of women's sport.

'If only I'd been born a fella' is a refrain you often hear from greats in women's sport, especially those outstanding players who flourished long before the media had started to pay attention. *I could've been a household name*, is the gist; *I would've been a hero to so many. Instead, I laboured in obscurity.* It speaks to the hold that patriarchy has on us all, in that it's sometimes easier for us to imagine being men than to imagine a world where female sporting achievement is held in equal esteem.

It's October 2019. The camogie season is over until January and the bruises on my arms and legs have begun their retreat for another winter. Without the benefit of training three times a week, I'll keep myself ticking over in the gym. I'm not a huge fan of working out; I prefer to exercise with the distraction of a ball to chase after, and at the gym I find it difficult to focus on anything but my own discomfort. But if I want to retain even a modicum of fitness over the winter, the gym is the easiest option.

(And look, it's not just about fitness. Growing up, camogie always kept me toned, lent my body a tightness and a leanness. But I'm older now; my summer body doesn't quite carry me through the winter. I like a glass of wine and a wedge of brie. I'm softening around the edges.)

I would like to go unseen in the gym. I would like to pop in my headphones, stare at the wall as I warm up on the elliptical, and then cycle between the weight machines without ever speaking or indeed making eye contact with any other patron. The brightly coloured jerseys and O'Neill's togs that I wear on the camogie pitch will attract too much attention, I think. I need a gym uniform, and that means fitting in with all the other women. It means leggings and vests. It means athleisure.

The flagship Life Style Sports I visit is on Grand Parade in Cork city, on the site of the former Capitol cinema. The store itself is a strange mix of nightclub, warehouse, workout studio and retail outlet, and seems designed to spike one's heart rate (and cortisol levels): fluorescent lights, neon signs, exposed pipework, mirrored surfaces, workout playlists thudding through the speakers. The runners are displayed on miniature podiums like works of art. Even the mannequins give the impression of being too cool to hang with you.

I make my way to the Women's Studio upstairs, which is its own intimate little section: less intimidating and stimulating than the rest. Pastel signs with motivational quotes are shelved alongside the merchandise, the exercise equivalents of 'Live, laugh, love.' They seem harmless enough, until I stop dead in front of one: 'Happiness is expensive.' I look around me, at the adjacent rack of Nike clothing: their Hyper Femme hoodie costs €70, while their Sculpt Victory leggings will set you back €50. I can't decide if I'm impressed at the store's self-awareness or astonished by the brazenness.

The Women's Studio encapsulates how exercise is packaged, marketed and commodified for women. If we run with the contextual implication that happiness is keeping fit, then to achieve that happiness you have to spend money – on products that urge us to be Hyper Femme, even as we're physically pushing ourselves. Our very leggings are reminding us to Sculpt our wobbly thighs to Victory. Happiness is expensive, and exercise for women is still hopelessly wrapped up in the beauty industry – even in this supposedly progressive strong-not-skinny age.

Though fitness influencers are careful not to focus on weight loss these days, the implicit goal is still to become perfectly lean and toned. The concept of penance clings to exercise – maybe especially in the case of women. It's transactional: in order to enjoy chocolate, takeaways or wine, one must burn off the corresponding number of calories in the gym. 'I'm being good because I'm going on holidays next week,' a friend of mine says, refusing a second slice of pizza. Even holidays – a break from normal life, a time to rest and recharge – have become a sort of performance for women, one that requires extensive preparation.

After winning the Euros in 2022, the England women's soccer team revealed that they had made a case to Nike, the manufacturers of their team kit, to replace the shorts of their traditional all-white strip with a darker pair, citing anxiety experienced by their players while on their periods.

'It's something we've fed back to Nike,' said Beth Mead, who was Player of the Tournament at the Euros. 'It's very nice to have an all-white kit but sometimes it's not practical when it's the time of the month. We deal with it as best we can.'

Tennis players also came forward with their experiences, especially of playing at Wimbledon, with its all-white dress code and limited bathroom breaks, while menstruating. Heather Watson told *The Times*: 'I have come off court and I've looked and gone: "Oh my God. I hope you can't see that in any pictures."' Alicia Barnett, meanwhile, spoke of how being on her period affected her game: 'Your body feels looser, your tendons get looser, sometimes you feel like you're a lot more fatigued. Sometimes your coordination just feels really off, and for me I feel really down and it's hard to get that motivation. Obviously, you're trying to play world-class tennis but it's really hard when you're PMS-ing and you feel bloated and tired.'

The Women's Super League is also increasingly address-ing this issue, with West Brom switching from white to navy shorts in September 2022, and Chelsea actively tak-ing players' menstrual cycles into consideration when planning training sessions since 2020. The Antrim ladies' football team, managed by two women – Emma Kelly and Kyla Trainor – have also changed their togs from white to green, and have a policy of open communication with their players about pain management during their cycles.

One might posit that in a truly progressive and feminist society, women would not care about visible menstrual blood on their shorts, at least no more than they worry about any other bloodstain on their kit. But we don't live in that world. Whether it's jokes about PMS and mood swings making women unsuitable for leadership, a former US president disparaging a female journalist with the words 'blood coming out of her whatever', or the men-strual pad brand Always using blue liquid in their ads to represent period blood, women are still made to feel shame about their periods.

I have an acute memory of being in the Square shop-ping centre in Tallaght as a fourteen-year-old, wearing light-coloured chequered pants, when my period arrived unexpectedly. I was able to buy pads in the shopping centre, but I couldn't quite stretch to a new pair of trou-sers. I'll never forget the sense of exposure as I walked around in public, as if my skin had been peeled back. Most women I know have a similar horror story from their teen years: it is archetypal. It's this same well of old anxiety and shame that plays on sportswomen's minds when they pull on white shorts at that time of the month.

There is a beige mark on the inside of my helmet, on the white foam where my forehead rests. I've tried cleaning it but, like the Turin shroud, it's permanently marked: the result of dozens of my nine-to-five faces being sweated out on the evening training pitch. It makes me think of Pat Comer's excellent documentary *Blues Sisters*, which followed the Dublin ladies' football squad through their All-Ireland-winning 2017 season. In one scene, county secretary (and jersey-washer-in-chief) Kathleen Colreavy lamented the jersey design: 'When I saw the white collar on these jerseys I nearly died. I was thinking of makeup, fake tan. You'd know 'twas men designed the jerseys, wouldn't you.' Perhaps if women's jerseys were designed by women – or, indeed, if men were more likely to be in the role of jersey-washer – collars would be dark in colour by default.

Athleisure makeup is an increasingly popular subset of cosmetics that promises not to slide off your face when you exercise. MAC's version is called Work It Out; Penneys' is No Sweat. When I see these products, I feel torn. On the one hand, I know that for many women, referring to makeup as 'warpaint' is not a joke: it's literal armour for getting through the day in a culture where women are constantly judged on their appearance. Going to the gym can be intimidating at the best of times; with the bright lights, mirrors and Lycra, there is a very real sense that you're on display. If having a full face of makeup on alleviates that pressure, what harm?

Another part of me is dismayed by the very existence

of athleisure makeup, since sport is one of the few contexts in which women can claim a public, physical presence that is separate from beauty. Even when a woman's public role is ostensibly not about their looks – politics or journalism, say – the issue will rear its perfectly-contoured head. Too feminine, and she can't be taken seriously. ('You looked like a two-bit hooker,' read one email to Australian journalist Annabel Crabb following a 2013 TV appearance.) Not feminine or manicured enough, and she's either not making an effort or being deceitful about her gender or sexuality. (Listen to style guru Tim Gunn's 2010 comments on Hillary Clinton's pantsuits: 'I think she's confused about her gender.')

I want to believe that sport is the one context of contemporary life in which the overwhelming pressure on women to present themselves attractively – to blend, to contour, to pluck, to bleach, to suck in, to touch up, to grin and bear it – is lifted, in favour of the more primal visibility of simply being a body at play. Camogie has the potential to be especially freeing in this way, since your face and hair – the two primary signifiers of the feminine beauty ideal – are obscured by a helmet. It's hard to either denigrate or objectify what little can be seen through the bars of a faceguard.

But the idea that the kinetic poetry of a female body excelling in sport would somehow circumvent misogyny doesn't, unfortunately, hold up to scrutiny. The physical genius of Serena Williams, Caster Semenya, Marion Bartoli and other top female athletes hasn't prevented their looks from being scrutinized and disparaged. When a stunning photo of Australian rules footballer Tayla Harris, captured airborne and mid-kick, appeared on social media in March 2019, it was met with a barrage of misogynistic comments. This is sexism at work: find an image of female physical power, and turn that very power back on the subject to humiliate her.

Is it any wonder that young women drop out of sport in their droves when images of women in sport are dissected and mocked in this way? Playing sport as a teenage girl already involves going against the overwhelming pressure from society to be feminine, quiet, and not to take up too much space.

'The vast majority of WNBA players lack crossover sex appeal,' ESPN sports pundit Bill Simmons wrote in 2006. 'The baggy uniforms don't help.' For it to be worth men's while to watch women's sports, the implication seems to be, the players can't just be talented at their chosen sport – they need to look good doing it.

Appearance, not performance, is often the driving force behind the design of women's athletic gear. Holly Bradshaw, the British pole vaulter and Olympic bronze medallist, wrestled with this unfortunate fact when she arrived in Tokyo in July 2021 for the Olympic Games. Normally for competitions she wore an all-in-one suit with knee-length shorts, but the standard-issue Team GB gear she was given consisted of briefs and crop tops.

'In my head, I was panicking,' she told *The Telegraph*. 'I didn't want to go to the most important competition of my life and not feel comfortable because I was worried about what I would be wearing.'

The sexist double standard struck her, too. Male pole vaulters wear Lycra shorts and tank tops: sleek enough to get them cleanly over the bar, but with coverage, too. Why weren't they expected to flash their stomachs and thighs, like their female counterparts? Early in her career, Bradshaw had been subject to social media abuse: strangers criticizing her body and calling her out of shape, even as she represented her country at elite level. She felt that the bikini-style Olympics uniform invited this sort of scrutiny and criticism.

Bradshaw voiced her concerns, and Team GB compromised, allowing her to compete in a rowing uniform that was more along the lines of what she usually wore. But Bradshaw was a twenty-nine-year-old at her third Olympics: she felt confident, established, and secure enough to question the higher-ups. Would a young athlete, just coming into the sport, feel as capable of pushing back? Or would she just put up with it, telling herself that this is just the way things are?

In camogie – but not, interestingly, in ladies' football – skorts, rather than shorts, are compulsory for all matches. They are not uncomfortable; nor do they impede performance. But rather than an accommodation to the female body – like dark shorts – the skort is merely a signifier of femaleness, a message to the observer rather than an adaptation to the player. As Dublin camogie player Eve O'Brien told The42.ie in 2018: 'We wear skorts just because we're women – it's feminine and we should be ladies and wear skorts. It's a small thing but it's very symbolic of the organisation that is quite traditional.' Like the 'ladies' in ladies' football, the skort feels like nothing more than an attempt to keep us in our box.

*

We don't yet have a female equivalent of the jock. Boys who play sport are in the happy position of having their masculinity and desirability enhanced by their sporting prowess. As a teenager, this bemused my teammates and me on nights out at provincial nightclubs: Tipperary county minors, no matter how gauche or ordinary-looking, were still highly sought after. On the other hand, try telling a boy that you were on the county camogie panel: at best he'd be pleasantly uninterested, at worst, vaguely disgusted.

Girls who play sport are pressurized to course-correct, to demonstrate that despite the unfortunate competitive streak that leads them to pursue sport, they're still feminine girly girls behind it all. So lather on the fake tan. Invest in a no-sweat foundation, the best you can afford. Put on tight-fitting yet effortless athleisure wear. Be strong, not skinny (but if skinny is a natural consequence of strong, what harm?). Be brilliant, but modest to a fault.

All of this takes up mental space and energy that male athletes simply don't have to bother with. Just as the playing pitch and the swimming pool are now the only places I don't bring my smartphone, they're also the only contexts where worrying about my appearance is futile, even counterproductive. When I play sport, my skin gets red and puffy. My hair gets lank and sweaty. My arms and legs become port-wine-stained with bruises. I have had to train myself not to care.

And yet, and yet. Team sport does something to a girl. I can say this because I've played this sport since I was old enough to hold a hurley, and it's only now, in my thirties, that I'm starting to fully appreciate all the ways in which camogie has shaped me.

You get to think about your body in terms of what it can do, rather than how it looks. You become more engine than ornament. Camogie is the only context in which I have ever been praised for aggression. It teaches you to be commanding, to take your ground. To assert, rather than mitigate, your physical presence. 'Win the dirty ball' was the mantra of a former coach of mine, and it's stuck in my head – get into the thick of it, where it's not pretty, and emerge with the ball in your hand. Slog is as necessary as skill. Perseverance is as essential as ability.

Team sport confers on women opportunities to face fears, take risks, and get hurt without serious consequences. Though I'm now a less skittish, nervy player than I was in my younger days, there are still things I fear on the pitch. I still get scared when I go in for a high ball. It's the lottery of it: the clash of bodies mid-air, the possibility of a broken hand, or of the unseen jab from behind when you're at full stretch and vulnerable. When I manage to pull off a catch, I'm unreasonably pleased on the basest of levels, like a Labrador after snagging a frisbee.

That same coach used to also say, 'The fear of winning can be as big as the fear of losing.' Winning, this coach was saying, creates expectations. Winning demands that you do better next time, win again and again. Losing is easy and comfortable; everyone knows how. Winning requires confidence, something which girls are typically socialized against at a young age. *Oh no, I'm desperate. State of me. Would you stop, it's from Penneys.* To win, you must believe you are deserving.

2. *Visibility*

I drive home to Tipp at the end of July for a dinner to celebrate my father's seventieth birthday. While there, I hope
to also sort through the boxes of keepsakes in the attic
that my mother has been gently reminding me about for
years.

Among the rubble of college notes, favourite childhood
books and old board games is a scrapbook with a *Thomas
the Tank Engine* cover. It's dated 1990, the year I began primary school, and titled 'My Tiqq Book'. Holding it is a
powerful experience, and I tell myself that I can remember making it – can remember cutting out, sticking in and
captioning the pictures. (The smell of old Pritt Stick is an
evocative thing.) I have one very specific image of lying on
my bedroom carpet and calling out to my father in another
room, asking him to spell some word or other. Whether
this memory is real or invented, I'm not sure.

The scrapbook begins, naturally, with a double-page
spread of Nicky English photos – some cut from news-
papers, some from match programmes, some from All-Star
posters. Many of the pictures are from Tipperary's All-
Ireland hurling final win over Antrim the previous year.
Nicky is followed by captain Bobby Ryan, the earliest GAA
player I can remember doing paid endorsements (farming
chemicals); Paul Delaney, who hurled with our neighbouring club Roscrea, and was one of the few players of that era
to wear a helmet (no faceguard); Bonnars Colm, Conal and
Cormac; Ryans Declan and Aidan (no relation); Pat Fox.
When I ran out of individual players I started improvising,

even resorting to other counties. 'Good Page. Tipp' reads one caption. 'Waterforb' reads another. 'A Big Nicky' is written on a page that contains, well, a large picture of Nicky English. A photo of the Artane Band is dubiously captioned 'The Panb'. On another page featuring a couple of team photos, I wrote 'Tiqq again'; then, as an afterthought: 'Gaillimh is well.' On an empty page – since no page could be left blank – I'd simply written 'Tipp Tipp hooray.'

After I pass it around to my family, and after we've all gotten a good laugh out of my four-year-old self's seriousness and dogged attempts at spelling, I feel a little melancholy. I am so distant from that kid who idolized Nicky and dreamed of winning All-Irelands with Tipp. I see the disconnect between that four-year-old's ambitions and what would be attainable for her in reality. In the scrapbook, there isn't a single woman.

Over the winter of 2016 and early 2017, I was working in an industrial estate in Little Island, just east of Cork city. Every day I drove from my small apartment in the city centre through Glanmire and Tivoli, out by the Marina and on to the N8. The drive was stressful and traffic-choked. Páirc Uí Chaoimh, closed for redevelopment for the previous two years, was sprouting again on the far bank of the river – a little higher each week, or so it seemed to me.

I was always either late for work or late for training, heightening my own driving anxiety by listening non-stop to true-crime podcasts. But throughout that winter, there was a moment on my route home that always lifted my spirits. On the Lower Glanmire Road, as I swung around the train station, was a billboard promoting Lidl's sponsorship of the Ladies Gaelic Football Association. It featured Briege Corkery and Sinéad Goldrick, dramatically lit and unsmiling, staring down the camera. Their hair was tied back, match-ready, and there were streaks of dirt on their faces. They looked powerful. They looked the way male athletes have always been portrayed: as icons of strength and prowess.

In 2003, when I was sixteen going on seventeen – just coming into myself as an adult player – the Camogie Association ran a campaign entitled 'Chicks with Sticks' as a way of promoting the game in its centenary year. The campaign was launched with an image of Dublin players Aoife Cullen, Eimear Brannigan and Sonya Byrne on the cover of the now-defunct *Fairplay* magazine, brandishing their hurleys and dressed as if for a night on the town. An *Irish Examiner* story about the Chicks campaign featured this quote from an unnamed Camogie Association spokesperson: 'Generally speaking, players are also more image conscious and desperately want to lose the burly, butch and brawny impression that is so often wrongly associated with the game.' So concerned was the Camogie Association with shrugging off its unglamorous rural roots that it overshot in the other direction.

Ireland of the 1990s and 2000s didn't quite know what to make of sportswomen, particularly in team sport. Anxieties over female physical prowess were manifested in different ways. Photoshoots with everyone pretty, smiling and unthreatening; All-Ireland fashion editorials in which players were asked about their fashion sense and shopping habits. I vividly remember reading, as a teenager, a straight-girl-undercover-at-a-lesbian-nightclub piece in a Sunday

broadsheet, in which the author marvelled over how feminine some of the women were, while others looked like
'subs on a camogie team'. A 2014 *Sunday Independent* article,
in which the journalist Niamh Horan joined a women's
rugby team for a training session, assured the reader,
'These are not butch, masculine, beer-swilling, men-hating
women.' This is the irony of playing team sport as a young
woman: while camogie is to a great extent responsible for
your self-assurance and positive body image, sometimes
you get a glimpse of how the rest of the world sees you,
and it catches you off-guard.

At a family gathering, my uncle Jack is telling me about his
1973 honeymoon with his late wife Orla, driving around
the Ring of Kerry.

'We had to delay it slightly because I had a match the
day after the wedding,' he says ruefully.

'What about Orla?' I ask. They were a GAA power
couple; Jack played hurling for Moneygall and Tipp, while
Orla played camogie for Austin Stacks in Clontarf and
Dublin. Both were All-Ireland winners.

'Oh, no. At that time, married women weren't allowed
to play for Dublin.'

I choke on my drink.

'She kept playing away for the club, of course, and even
represented Leinster, but she couldn't play for Dublin for
at least a year anyway, till they did away with that rule.'

It seems that Dublin camogie followed the same prin-
ciples as Ireland's 'marriage bar': a law that, until 1973,
meant that women employed in the public service had to
resign as soon as they got married.

'That's some compliment that she married you anyway,' I tell him.

He laughs. 'Ah well. That's romance.'

In 2015, writer Claire Vaye Watkins published an essay called 'On Pandering' in which she described growing up as an aspiring writer in an education system that held male writers and male experience to be inherently more literary, and more worthy of emulation, than their female equivalents. One section, titled 'Watching Boys Do Stuff', struck a chord:

> I've watched boys play the drums, guitar, sing, watched them play football, baseball, soccer, pool, Dungeons and Dragons and Magic: The Gathering. I've watched them golf. Just the other day I watched them play a kind of sweaty, book-nerd version of basketball. I've watched them work on their trucks and work on their master's theses. I've watched boys build things: half-pipes, bookshelves, screenplays, careers. I've watched boys skateboard, snowboard, act, bike, box, paint, fight, and drink. I could probably write my own series of six virtuosic autobiographical novels based solely on the years I spent watching boys play *Resident Evil* and *Tony Hawk's Pro Skater*. I watched boys in my leisure time, I watched boys in my love life, and I watched boys in my education.

Why do girls watch boys do stuff? Is it that we hope they will reciprocate? I remember being disabused of this notion in secondary school, when it quickly became apparent that the boys' athletic ability was impressive in a way that mine was not, because it was their role to be the doer and mine to be the passive admirer. While the courage and competence of men is very often a pleasure for women to behold – it certainly is for me, as a woman who watches hurling – that does not mean that the reverse is always true. Sometimes, the bravery and strength of women is received by men as a threat – a threat they can minimize by ignoring, ridiculing or excluding the woman in question.

I think of Watkins' essay when I see the small crowds that come to watch our games, to watch girls do stuff for a change. Most of them are parents, siblings and partners of the players.

'There's very little drama on camogie teams,' a former mentor said to me recently. His tone was puzzled; he was trying to reason it out. And he's right. Camogie teams rarely suffer from the issues that plague team sports – no egos, no feigned injuries, no mouthing off. There is a grim sense of getting on with it.

I'm tempted to suggest that camogie players don't engage in drama because we have no audience. But that's not quite true – the audience bit. Things are slowly getting better. A huge breakthrough was RTÉ's decision in 2016 to broadcast not just the camogie All-Ireland final – the only camogie match televised annually throughout my childhood – but the semi-finals, too. The following year, they went one better and showed the quarter-finals as well.

These days, the All-Ireland camogie final draws about a quarter of a million viewers and a crowd of about 25,000 – encouraging figures, but still dramatically smaller than the audiences for the men's finals, and only about half of what ladies' football attracts on its biggest day. This, perhaps, shows the impact of long-term media exposure: TG4 backed ladies' football early, televising most games since 1999, while camogie took almost two decades to catch up.

In Cork, the city where I live and play, murals of camogie stars Rena Buckley and Ashling Thompson adorn walls and electrical boxes alongside Christy Ring and Jimmy Barry Murphy. When I go to training three times a week at the Barrs, I see dozens of young girls out playing with their friends, competing with each other and expressing themselves. They will grow up seeing camogie on television as a matter of course. They will see intercounty players depicted on billboards and in street art. They'll make scrapbooks of their heroines, or some digital equivalent. They'll have no idea how far we've come.

3. Motherhood

It has become standard, at the end of All-Ireland finals in the men's codes, for players to bring their babies and toddlers on to the pitch after the game in a tiny mini-me jersey, sometimes even putting them – delightfully! – into the trophy itself. (Google 'baby in Sam Maguire' and thank me later.) This is a much rarer occurrence with female players of Gaelic games: most players retire before, or because, they have children. Kilkenny's Anne Dalton was a mother of three when she retired in 2021. She said frankly in an interview with *The Irish Times* that her wife, Karen, 'carried all the kids, hence why I'm still able to play camogie'.

*

It usually starts with a 'back injury'. A player will show up to training in her clothes, as they say. She'll stand on the sideline and watch the session, pitching in if necessary by working the keeper or striking in balls for a game of backs and forwards. But she won't take meaningful part in the session. She'll wince and say she did something to her back.

Once the first scan arrives and everything looks positive, the sheepish WhatsApp message can go out to the team: *Sorry everyone, my back is actually fine . . . I have a bit of news!* It's a tried and trusted template, deployed on every adult team I've played with. Everyone who has been around a while knows what 'back injury' means.

In sport, as in life, it's different for women. Many men can become parents without experiencing much disruption to their working or playing careers. Women, on the other hand, take leave from their jobs for the best part of a year, often returning with the expectation that they now need flexi-time, that they will be the ones to take a day of annual leave when their child is sick.

The body needs time to recover after giving birth, and between this and the demands of looking after a small baby, most new mothers will not be seen back on the pitch for at least a season. After giving birth to her daughter Doireann in April 2011, my sister Eileen made a huge effort to return to camogie training as soon as possible. But when her second daughter, Aoife, was born in April 2013, her schedule became more challenging. When Éanna arrived in September 2016, Eileen was flat out. As good as sport was for her physical and mental health, she decided that she had no option but to quit.

Eileen told me she 'couldn't justify coming in from work at half six to a baby and a toddler who hadn't seen me all day, then heading out the door half an hour later to training'. It was extremely difficult for her to walk away from the sport she loved. 'In hindsight I would say it took me about two years to come to terms with the decision. I found it very hard to even attend matches.'

Niamh Kerr, a footballer with St Jude's of Dublin, was thirty-four and a mother of one when St Jude's won the 2021 All-Ireland junior club final. In an interview with the *Irish Independent*, she described the 'guilt' of playing sport as a parent – something I don't think I've ever heard a male player express. 'I'll admit it, it's hard, it's much harder when you have a child,' said Kerr. 'You feel guilty for leaving. You could also be having a match after a night when you have had very little sleep and it's hard. You do have to rely on your partner and your friends and family. I have a very, very supportive partner, Richard knows how much I love playing.'

On the plus side, she reflected that she was setting a good example for her son. 'But it's great for Ben. I was thinking about the mental and physical benefits of playing football but you are teaching your kids life lessons without even realizing. They are seeing you be passionate about something. They are seeing you work and commit to something . . . There's such value in that.'

My sister Eileen, too, was drawn back to sport in part because of her kids. When Doireann and Aoife began playing with Moneygall underage, Eileen became a coach, picking up a hurley again for the first time in many years and rediscovering her love for the game. In 2020, she began training again herself with Moneygall, the kids now old enough to bring along to training and have their own puck-around on the sideline.

Eileen is part of a new generation of young female coaches who are also former players. This cohort was much smaller in the 1990s, when I was growing up. In fact, 2017, my first season playing with the Barrs, was the first time I'd ever had a female manager in almost two decades of adult hurling at multiple levels (club, county, school and college). There had often been female selectors; in camogie it's a requirement to have at least one woman on the selection team, someone to come into the dressing-room and ask 'Everyone decent?' before admitting the male manager to give the pre-match talk. But it had never been a woman *giving* the pre-match talk. Ellen Clifford, my first manager at the Barrs, had been a player until a few years previously; she'd been where we'd been, she knew what it was like. One practice match, when we were stuck for a goalie, she stood between the posts herself.

Just as the demands of motherhood are a factor in shortening players' careers, they also must work against the development of a large cohort of female coaches. As Meath footballer Vikki Wall pointed out in an interview with the *Irish Independent*, 'the age that men get into coaching is maybe the time that women are having families'. With many women struggling to combine a full-time career with the demands of motherhood, adding several hours a week of volunteering is not a reasonable prospect. Also implicit in Wall's comments is the understanding that many of those former male players in their late thirties and early forties who venture into management – who may also be new parents – are enabled to do so by wives who hold the fort at home.

4. *Integration*

On holidays abroad, it's always easy to spot your GAA fellow travellers. The headbands in county colours tied around the handles of wheelie suitcases, all the better to spot them on the baggage belt. In the line for security you're directly behind a kid shouldering a backpack they got at the previous summer's Cúl Camp. *The GAA*, it reads. *Where we all belong.* Afterwards, you come across this phrase everywhere. Bus shelter ads. Overheard on the radio. An emotive TV campaign. But it isn't strictly true.

The GAA was founded as, and remains, a fraternal organization. In its mission statement, the GAA's Official Guide states: 'The primary purpose of the G.A.A. is the organisation of native pastimes and the promotion of athletic fitness as a means to create a disciplined, self-reliant, national-minded manhood.' It goes on to describe one of its aims as 'consolidating our Irish identity', but it does so through games for boys and men only.

The Camogie Association and LGFA remain what they have always been: dramatically smaller organizations for promoting the same games among girls and women. Governance of the women's codes, on the whole, has been unsatisfactory. Year after year, the two women's organizations have failed to coordinate their fixture calendars, despite repeated calls for this action from the grassroots. This lack of coordination puts intercounty dual players in impossible situations where they are forced to pick one sport over the other. In 2020, motions to facilitate dual players were defeated at both the LGFA and Camogie Association's annual congresses, to the widespread frustration of players. The disconnect between the associations and the players they are supposed to serve was never more apparent.

But change is in motion. In 2018, the GAA's *Towards 2034* document explicitly stated the aim of having all Gaelic games under one umbrella by the time of the GAA's 150th anniversary. Then, in December 2020, the GPA (Gaelic Players' Association) and its female counterpart, the WGPA, voted near-unanimously to amalgamate – a heartening example of allyship from male players, who knew it was the right thing to do. As in any union, the members with the most power protect those with the least.

In February 2022, GPA co-chair Maria Kinsella proposed a motion at GAA Congress to unite the GAA, the LGFA and the Camogie Association. It was overwhelmingly supported from the floor. GAA president Larry McCarthy, managing expectations about the pace at which integration might realistically happen, observed: 'Corporate entities can come together relatively quickly, but you have three different cultural associations coming together.'

As I write this in October 2022, the steering group on integration, chaired by former president Mary McAleese, released a statement enshrining equality at the heart of the integration process: 'It was unanimously agreed that the future integrated structure will be based on One Association for all Gaelic games and built on the principle of equality.'

This represents a huge opportunity for the women's codes. One sporting body for both genders is not in itself a guarantee of equality – the FAI demonstrates that readily enough. But if equality is prioritized at the start of the process, then everything is on the table: equal allocation of resources and pitches, equal expense rates for all players, integrated fixture calendars and male/female double-headers.

Historically, there has been a certain amount of cooperation and goodwill between the GAA and its sister organizations, particularly at a grassroots club level. This relationship has always been informal, with the terms 'related organizations' and 'affiliates' variously being used to describe the links. On the Camogie Association website, the GAA is listed as one of the body's 'sponsors'. In the run-up to integration talks, however, the ties have become more formalized – such as the announcement, in late 2021, that the GAA would oversee the Camogie Association's commercial rights, including TV broadcast rights and sponsorship, for an initial three-year period.

From an equality standpoint, access to playing pitches is one of the most urgent issues. The vast majority of Gaelic games pitches in the country are owned by GAA clubs. Women and girls have in some cases been forced to pay for access to county GAA grounds, and have to live with the ever-present danger of being unceremoniously turfed out at the last minute. The most egregious recent example occurred in December 2020, during the wintertime pandemic championships. The ladies' football All-Ireland semi-final between Cork and Galway was originally fixed for late November in Semple Stadium, but was changed to 6 December in the Gaelic Grounds in Limerick, to avoid a fixture clash for

Cork's dual players. However, as soon as the Limerick hurlers qualified for the All-Ireland hurling final, the ladies' footballers were informed that the Gaelic Grounds was no longer available for their fixture: the Limerick men needed it for training.

The semi-final was switched to Parnell Park in Dublin – but the pitch there turned out to be frozen over, and so at the last minute the game was moved to Croke Park. Great, you might think – except the venue was changed so hastily that a TV broadcast could not be arranged in time, and Galway arrived at the stadium late, giving them little time to prepare. It was, in short, a mess.

A striking trend in the wake of this fiasco was how quickly LGFA officials moved to praise the GAA for facilitating them, seeming grateful for any crumbs from the GAA table. The incoming LGFA president, Mícheál Naughton, said: 'our association would not be in existence if it were not for the men giving us grounds and pitches. For that we are very grateful.' This is consistent with a general sense that if women kick up too much, or set the bar of expectations higher, we'll lose what mutual understandings and tentative agreements we have. The LGFA, by far the youngest of the three bodies, has been more effective than the Camogie Association in establishing visibility, media attention and sponsorship. But as we enter a serious process of planning the integration of Gaelic games, we'll need to be more assertive.

Might women be sidelined in a unified GAA? Or conversely, might there be unease and backlash if men perceive themselves to be losing power and resources as the association works to achieve better gender balance? The administrators of the women's organizations, for their part, may fear that for all that women have to gain from integration, they have something to lose, too – independence, branding, the unique and distinct histories they have carved out as organizations dedicated solely to women's sport. They will no doubt want to protect existing partnerships (such as the LFGA's broadcast agreement with TG4, which has hugely benefited both) and rulebook quirks (skorts, the countdown clock and siren). Integration is not subsumption, after all, and one assumes that there will be give and take, that it will be possible to retain some of the old in the brave new world.

Integration is also an interesting opportunity to dust down those traditions and see if they are still fit for purpose in the twenty-first century. Nomenclature is not even on the integration agenda, as far as I know, but will it make sense to continue to refer to hurling played by women as 'camogie' and Gaelic football played by women as 'ladies' football'? The latter, in particular, has never sounded right: if it is women's tennis, women's athletics, women's soccer, then why 'ladies' Gaelic football'? (In Irish, the LGFA is rendered as *Cumann Peil Gael na mBan*, or 'women's Gaelic football association'.) 'Camogie' at least has the advantage of being its own unique word, even if, in the OED, it's defined as 'an Irish game resembling hurling, played by women or girls'. It no longer merely resembles hurling: they are basically the same sport. And if, in order to explain what camogie is, you have to say the word 'hurling' anyhow, then why not just call it women's hurling?

In the integration process, there is everything to play for, and we have to make sure that life in a unified GAA will be better for girls and women. As former GAA president Liam O'Neill has said: 'If we were designing the GAA now we would not design what we have.' Women would be involved from the ground floor up, not tacked on at the end. In fact, when it comes to kids, the GAA already is quite gender-inclusive; at underage levels, groups of girls train happily alongside groups of boys, with equal access to pitches and supports. When you look at it through the lens of kids, it's indefensible to say that our sons have a birthright to the GAA and all its resources but our daughters don't.

In March 2021, at the launch of an AIG virtual gym for club players training on their own, Dublin camogie player Ali Twomey performed the sort of PR high-wire act that has become second nature to female players whenever they are invited to the launch of a competition, jersey or sponsorship deal. They show up, gamely pose for photos, and then talk to the media about systemic inequalities and the frustrations of being a female intercounty player. Never mind what the presser is ostensibly about; the goal is to maximize the platform to talk about bread-and-butter issues.

Twomey expounded on the status of female players compared to their male counterparts. Like the men, female intercounty players now effectively live and train like professionals. But unlike the men, women receive no compensation for expenses, and they cannot count on decent provision of gear or post-training food. Before I heard Twomey speak on this, I had made a lot of assumptions about the conditions under which Dublin's female players operated. That AIG logo emblazoned across all four jerseys – hurling, football, camogie and ladies' football – projects a sense of equity, of shared resources. It was a model for other counties to emulate, I thought. I also assumed that Dublin players would escape much of the travel expenditure that other intercounty players, who might have to leave their county of origin for work or study, incur on a weekly basis. But Twomey pointed out that she paid €100 a month just for tolls to get to training. None of that could be claimed back.

It always delights me and makes me wince in equal measure, these frank admissions from high-performing female players. Doing their promo duty, smiling for the camera, then talking about what's making their blood boil. It speaks to a very particular kind of resilience: how to keep turning up, year after year, to a sport that you love but which is also plainly unfair. How to manage your justifiable anger.

On an episode of *Off the Ball* in June 2019, Cork footballer Doireann O'Sullivan shocked her male co-panellists by revealing that she has never received mileage or expenses for playing for her county. Likewise, in May 2022, Mayo great Fiona McHale tweeted: 'Can confirm LGFA players DO NOT get expenses. If I were to claim mileage the way the men do, my weekly travel expenses would be €474.50.' Contrast this with a 2017 episode of *The GAA Hour* podcast from SportsJoe.ie. Former Laois footballer Colm Parkinson said: 'Genuinely, my commute from Dublin to Laois for training, I used to be hitting maybe a thousand quid a month on expenses coming down three nights a week. It is a great earner and that's tax free. It's a super few quid at the end of the month . . . We'd carpool down in four so only one car is doing the bulk of the driving but we all put in for four separate expenses. So I was getting a nice few quid out of these expenses. They've tightened up on that now.'

Some injustices are slowly being corrected. In May 2021, female intercounty players finally had their individual government grants brought into line with those of male hurlers and footballers. The women now receive €1,200 each from the government annually, just like the men; previously, they had only received €400 per year. But even €1,200 comes nowhere near covering travel commitments for many players, and until female intercounty players are relieved of the money stress incurred by simply excelling at their sport, it will remain one of the most glaring inequalities in Gaelic games. If, in one GAA for everyone, solving this problem means using the income streams from the male intercounty game to subsidize female development, then so be it.

There exists a scale of sexism towards women's sport. There are those who are quite frank about their aversion to watching women play, such as the *Sports Illustrated* contributor Andy Benoit, who once tweeted, 'Women's sports in general not worth watching.' At least those guys are upfront about it.

Perhaps a more insidious issue is – somewhat counter-intuitively – good men, who consider themselves feminists and support women's sport in theory but would never do anything as humble or practical as attend a women's sports event. Sexism – not active, malignant sexism, but a sort of passive, we-just-didn't-think-of-it sexism – is still a systemic factor that affects women's sports. There are still hurling fans who would never dream of watching a camogie match because 'the standard isn't as high'. These same fans will enthusiastically support their local boys' under-12s or junior B team without noticing any contradiction. It comes back to the stories we tell ourselves. Hurling fans can project their hopes on to a twelve-year-old boy, and see a future senior star in the making. They can look at the struggling junior B player and identify with him. But they're not used to watching women. They have no context for that.

Will men watch women? But that's not really the question. The question is, can men identify with women? Can they admire them? Especially if said women are not their mothers, wives or daughters?

13. Why We Do It

'Are you still at the camogie?'

It's a question that comes up a lot, over the Christmas break. You might meet cousins or schoolfriends or college friends who haven't seen you in a while. You're trying to place each other, colour in the sketched outline: jobs and partners and kids and cities of residence. And sport.

'Ah yeah, still going,' you say.

You see them do the mental arithmetic. Chances are they know the year you finished school, or graduated college, or played minor. It's a while back now.

Apropos of nothing, you bring up Pauline McCarthy, the unstoppable sixty-two-year-old who scored a goal in the Limerick junior B ladies' football final in November 2021. 'Lots of people put pressure on you but why should you give up something if you like doing it?' she told the *Limerick Leader* after helping St Ailbe's to victory. But Pauline is an outlier.

To be fair, it's a question worth asking. You love the sport despite the bruises, the rainy training sessions, the sometimes crushing disappointments and the general lack of fanfare. You've put in a fair amount of years. Will you do another?

There is a sense of unfinished business. An eminently avoidable injury interrupted your most recent season. You have to tell a succession of nurses, doctors, physios, friends and teammates how you came by this injury, and the embarrassment does not diminish with each telling. Suffice to say, your skateboarding days are over.

You're astonished by the young talent coming through in your club – how fearless they are, how calm under pressure. That enviable injection of pace. And then there's the visible strength of today's intercounty stars, years of quality S&C under their belts. The routines posted to Instagram: dumbbells, Gym+Coffee, dog-walking, sea-swimming. Entire lives geared towards excellence. You were never that disciplined, not even when you were their age. Could you be that disciplined now?

The first set of physio exercises were very modest in scope. You think of that scene in *Kill Bill*, where Uma Thurman is in the back of a car after waking up from a coma, trying to wiggle her big toe. It's not quite as bad as all that, but when you've been in a cast for six weeks, you begin to depersonalize your injured limb. Encased in plaster, you can't see it, and you can't manoeuvre it without using your hands or crutches; it no longer feels yours. That first set of exercises is all about becoming reacquainted. Rotating the joint as much as you can. Moving it from left to right, as far as it will go, imitating the movement of windscreen wipers. And yes, lots of toe-wiggling.

You are told your dorsiflexion will never be the same. It means you can't really squat any more, or move your knee forward over your toes: your ankle arrests the movement.

'It's great that you're still fairly young and fit,' your physio tells you, 'it'll help your recovery.' And you are lucky in that respect, but in hurling years, you're old. Perspective is everything.

Even on the day you get your cast off, you need your crutches to get up the stairs. After only six weeks, you trust the crutches more than your own two feet.

It comes back slowly, the trust. The sole of your repaired foot gets pins and needles when you put it flush to the floor, no longer used to that sort of contact. You can stand, but walking feels much harder. It means putting most of your weight on the dodgy foot. You laugh out loud in the kitchen when you take your new first steps, startling the cat.

Walking, swimming, cycling. They all come back eventually. Your physio tells you it's time to try running but you're afraid, afraid, afraid. You tried it once on the treadmill in the gym and you were convinced your foot was going to shatter. You know it's all in your head, this feeling, but it still causes your heart to judder in your chest. It's wild, the effect that the brain can have on the body.

At your parents' house, on the big lawn out the back with the two dogs flying everywhere, you make yourself run. It's not pretty, but it's a start.

You used to be very cynical, but as you've got older you increasingly find yourself welling up at books, movies, poignant Christmas ads. You do a bit of yoga and meditation. You read the odd self-help book.

One of these is *Daring Greatly* by Brené Brown, which takes its title from a speech by Theodore Roosevelt, the first and lesser of the Roosevelt presidents: 'It is not the critic who counts; not the man who points out how the strong man stumbles, or where the doer of deeds could have done them better. The credit belongs to the man who is actually in the arena, whose face is marred by dust and sweat and blood . . . who at the worst, if he fails, at least fails while daring greatly, so that his place shall never be with those cold and timid souls who neither know victory nor defeat.'

Like 'The Hurler's Prayer' from your childhood, Roosevelt's speech addresses 'the man' – but you still find it moving. Maybe it's not self-defeating to pursue something where you're constantly coming up short. Maybe it's daring greatly.

Ciarán Murphy of the *Second Captains* podcast, himself an ageing Gaelic footballer, gets it. Weighing up his own retirement in *The Irish Times*, he wrote:

> There are, of course, plenty of people in this very situation this Christmas. Sitting at home, wondering if 2020 and 2021 weren't crappy years to finish out on, with no dressing-rooms, shortened seasons, restrictions everywhere, Zoom quizzes, Covid questionnaires, the whole crummy gamut. Maybe if we got one full, uninterrupted year, you could walk away then, head held high . . . And then there's a county quarter-final on the line, you're a point down with three minutes to go, the ball comes into your corner, and you remind yourself – the game is the thing. Just the sheer thrill of it. There are no crowds, no external motivations, nothing beyond what you put into it. Just the game. You'll be long enough retired, as the old saying goes.

'How do you describe feelings?' Former Clare hurler and manager Ger Loughnane posed this question when interviewed for *The Game*, the 2018 hurling documentary. I also appear in *The Game* and so have never been able to watch it all the way through, but Loughnane's words are so incisive that they are heard in each episode's opening sequence. It's a question that writers grapple with every day at their desks.

I'm a writer and a camogie player, and I struggle to reconcile the two roles. Both are lovely and largely useless. Both are done primarily for their own sake, not for profit or fame. The only certainty of both disciplines is that you'll never master them.

How do you describe feelings? How, indeed.

We don't do it with any expectation of glory. Success in hurling is largely dependent on an accident of birth. If a talented player has the good fortune to be born in Tipp or Kilkenny or Cork or Limerick, they stand a good chance of winning All-Irelands in their career. If, on the other hand, they're born in Antrim, Laois, Westmeath or Carlow – or even in a county with a strong tradition but few titles, such as Waterford or Wexford – their chance of ultimate success is much lower, no matter how talented they are.

We don't do it for money, either. We're currently in an era of GAA history that we might one day look back on and say that players were an exploited class. Yes, the GPA does a good job of advocating for players' interests. Male intercounty players have their expenses covered, and big names in the sport might do well out of endorsement deals or media opportunities. But most intercounty players are still returning to a day job the Monday after the big game, and have their evenings and weekends hoovered up by training, whether with club or county. As standards and expectations become ever more professional, players are still expected to give their time and commitment for free, essentially fulfilling two full-time roles. Being a county player is a year-round pursuit now, and its demands permeate every aspect of the player's life – diet, work, leisure and family time. At the very least, a work-life balance crisis is looming in the GAA.

Despite our unshakeable faith in the uniqueness of GAA, there is little belief that we can create a bespoke professionalism that works for us. Ironically, the word 'professional' is used all the time in the GAA, and admiringly, to describe a 'professional setup' or 'professional standards'. I do it myself. We use this word with abandon, always with the understanding that we will never actually follow through on its meaning.

The time may be fast approaching when intercounty players will not be able to manage it all. Is there a way to lift some of their economic burden and let them focus on the game they love? The GAA has always found ways around amateurism: keep the lads in college with lucrative sports scholarships; find them handy jobs where frequent absences will be overlooked; overestimate their expense claims. It's important, now and in the future, to support players – male and female – in a more open and transparent way.

There is a part of you that does it to honour something. Your father, your father's father, your father's father's father. (It would be great to have foremothers too, but forefathers are all you have to work with.) You don't play in the club colours any more but there is a part of you that's playing for your dad, and for the long-ago memory of your grandfather watching from the diagonal wall at the pitch where you learned to play. You can still feel the weight of his gaze, but it's not a burdensome thing. It's a comfort.

It took you a long time to learn how to put a grip on your hurley. Your dad used to have to do it for you, but now your hands' movements are practised, unthinking. It's like learning to plait hair. You start at the top, just under the butt, the little protruding ridge that stops your hand from flying off the handle, that locks your grip when you have to lengthen the hurley suddenly – to pull on the ball, or to reach for it. You unpeel the backing off the grip and adhere it to the handle. They're foam these days, the grips, in neon colours; you remember when they were more towel-like. You unfurl it slowly, gradually peeling off the backing, placing it so that it overlaps a little on the preceding rotation, but not too much. You unwind it slowly, in a motion that describes a strand of DNA. A helix.

The DNA is good or *the DNA is strong* is something that is often said, carelessly, by hurling commentators or fans, about players whose mothers and fathers were themselves accomplished hurlers. My cousin Shane Ryan, for example, who played senior football and hurling for Dublin, winning six Leinster titles and a national league: his dad is Jack Ryan, my uncle, who won a hurling All-Ireland with Tipp in 1971, and his mother was the great Orla Ní Shíocháin, who won three camogie All-Irelands with Dublin. I have heard it said about Conor Browne of Kilkenny, whose mother and aunt are Angela Downey-Browne and Ann Downey, of Kilkenny camogie fame; of Mark McHugh, the Au-Ireland winning Donegal footballer, whose father Martin McHugh preceded him in that achievement. I don't think people mean any harm by it, but it perfectly taps into the sense of ownership that we on the inside of the GAA feel, that can sometimes come across as obnoxious cliquiness to those on the outside; like you have to be born to it, like it can't be learned –

Now you've messed up. Unwind and start again.

Sport changes how you interact with the world, in ways large and small. You hold the hurley in your dominant hand and catch the ball in the other. This lends itself, over the years, to a mild ambidexterity – or more accurately, a tendency to use the right hand for force and the left for finesse.

Unfortunately, not all skills are transferable. I can get the ball on the 45 with my back to goal and know instinctively which way to pivot. Even when marked, I can gravitate towards pockets of space. But can I parallel park?

To play camogie, for me, is to feel present, and have presence, in the world. To manipulate and impact the space around me. To wield power. There is something very thrilling to me about the directness of sport: how you go towards the ball, towards danger, especially when so much of navigating public space for women means avoiding, skirting, mitigating.

Sport is a chance to unlearn those behaviours that make me feel that I am not at home in the world. Get a taxi home; or, if you must walk, walk without earphones, your bunch of keys clenched in your fist. When parked on the street, and an unknown man is walking towards you, put on the central locking – just in case. Ingrained, automatic behaviours.

When Cal and I hold hands on a street at night, it's clear how differently we were socialized. While he walks directly, going to his destination as the crow flies, I am side-stepping the crowds, giving way – just in case. I end up dragging him off course, or letting go altogether. In our approaches to navigating public space, we are literally out of step.

But on the pitch? I can jostle or impede an opponent and not apologize or feel afraid. I spend so much of my life making myself small. In sport, I get to make myself big.

Beyond this: so much of regular life is spent repelling rain, avoiding muddy grass, blocking out ambient noise with earphones – whereas camogie is about leaning into the conditions. Negotiating with the environment rather than resisting it. The ground is hard, so watch the bounce. The grass is wet, so be sure of your pick. Listening to the shrill whistle, to the shouts of your coaches and team-mates as they let you know where they are, what they need. Lying on your back on wet grass to stretch as drizzle comes down, caught by the floodlights. Beginning a sprint from a prone position, blades of grass poking through your face-guard. The smell of the earth. You can't call it a connection with nature; a GAA pitch is as artificial as any golf course or tennis court. But it's a rooting of – and awareness of – one's body in the physical environment. And yes, it makes me feel alive.

*

People ask when I will have kids of my own. At the time of writing, I'm thirty-six and have been with my partner for almost a decade. I have a fourteen-year-old stepson who recently moved to Cork to live with us full-time and finish out his secondary education. I remember the first time I saw him, through a window, walking up a Dublin street to the coffee-shop where I was waiting to be introduced. Then, he had to reach up to hold his father's hand. Now he's a head taller than me.

When he's in Cork, he gets dragged to matches and gamely pucks around at half-time, this sport he was not born into but still enjoys. It makes me absurdly proud. I don't know if I want kids of my own, but the urge to pass the hurling torch is there just the same.

It's the time, of course. If I have a child, will I have the space in my brain for anything besides nurturing? Several of my teammates have kids and are still playing to a high standard. Lynda had her daughter, Darcy, at thirty-nine, during the first lockdown, and weeks later was back at the Lough doing sprints; I admired her from afar on my daily sanity walk. It can be done. But not every woman has to, I remind myself.

It can feel miraculous, that's the thing. When you're somehow able to calibrate your arms to the correct pitch and angle to strike a point, all in a split second, all without thinking. When your marker takes a touch too many and you flick the ball away and catch it cleanly, turning the impetus of play, you feel a sense of perfection in yourself: ludicrous, but real. When you stretch for a high ball, eyes closed, the length of you exposed and vulnerable, and still your fingers find the ball, close tight around it. When you're out of options and play the ball into your blind spot, and it falls within the wingspan of a patient teammate, who calmly collects and casts it over the bar.

The poet Billy Ramsell puts it brilliantly in 'Lament for Christy Ring': *He swerves, ducks his shoulder, elegantly jerks. / And what gap now between thought and act, / his spirit and firmware fusing?*

Maybe you can only say these things about the greats of the sport. What the rest of us do is smaller, humbler. But still, in the end, it's the best thing I know how to do.

It's the first spring after lockdown, and we are finally allowed in dressing-rooms again. I am only back training properly a few weeks. My ankle is healed, strong as ever, but the muscles surrounding it are still feeling the effects of the cast. I am comically slow at running. With each step, a stringy jolt of discomfort up the inside of my right leg. I think of it as a bum note, like interference on the radio, some overstretched or underpowered tendon creaking with the effort of propelling me forward.

Tonight is a junior match, and I'm wearing number 17. Our junior team is strong, a mixture of experienced players on the fringes of the senior team and young, emerging talent. Most of the players sitting in the dugout with me are half my age. By half-time, we're winning well, and Colette, the manager, asks if I'm happy to go on. I take this for the kindness it is: I'm nervous but I need the game time. There's only one way to know if you're match-fit, and it's by playing.

It takes me a while to settle, to tune into the pace of the

game. Junior is not as frantic as senior and this suits my current condition. I hit a wide, a couple of attempted passes go astray. But I know from experience that you just need one good moment to get back on track.

It comes ten minutes from time: a good ball struck in from midfield, head height. I put up the paw, latch on. I am suddenly, deliriously aware there is open space between me and the goal, and I lurch into this vacuum. I have only the goalie to beat, and am hit by the beautiful certainty that I will bury it. I already have the spot picked out.

Acknowledgements

Thank you to Kevin Barry and Olivia Smith at *Winter Papers,* who gave me the confidence and encouragement to write about camogie and the GAA.

A huge thanks to Lucy Luck, and to everyone at Sandy-cove, especially Brendan Barrington for his enthusiasm, wisdom and care.

I'm grateful to the Arts Council for awarding me funding to work on this project at a crucial stage in its development. Thanks also to everyone in the School of English at UCC, where I wrote much of this book as writer in residence.

Thank you to Iseult Howlett for adapting my essay 'The Fear of Winning' into the beautiful short film *The Grass Ceiling* (Kennedy Films, 2019), and for allowing me to borrow the great title.

Thanks to the crew at the *Irish Examiner* sports desk, especially Tony Leen, Colm O'Connor, Larry Ryan and Michael Moynihan. Thanks also to Adrian Russell for commissioning 'Sidestep' for The42.ie.

Thank you to the following friends who provided encouragement, advice and pep talks along the way: Laura Cassidy, Tadhg Coakley, Danny Denton, Pam Finn, Sinéad Gleeson, Ailbhe Ní Ghearbhuigh, Patrick O'Donoghue and Billy Ramsell. A huge thanks also to the wider Ryan family, especially those who feature as characters in these pages.

ACKNOWLEDGEMENTS

Thank you to my teammates and mentors, past and present, especially my friends at Moneygall and St Finbarr's. It's been an honour and a pleasure.

To my Cork family, Cal and Seb, and my Tipp family, Ber, Séamus, Conor, Eileen, Denis, Doireann, Aoife and Éanna – thanks for everything, with love.